KHUSHWANT SINGH (80), nove
much the most widely read columnist
columns are reproduced by over 50

With 64 books to his credit, Khushwant Singh first shot into fame with his award-winning bestseller *Train to Pakistan* (1955), which powerfully depicted the mass hysteria and senseless communal violence that followed the 1947 partition of the country. This novel was followed by *I Shall Not Hear the Nightingale (1959),* a short-story collection *A Bride for the Sahib* (1967), and the non-fiction work *Good People, Bad People* (1977).

Over the years he has lectured and written extensively on history, culture, and philosophy. In 1966, he published a two-volume *History of the Sikhs,* which has now been fully updated, and is still considered the most authoritative writing on the subject. His two recent bestsellers are *Sex, Scotch & Scholarship* and *Need for a New Religion in India and Other Essays.*

WOMEN & MEN IN MY LIFE

KHUSHWANT SINGH

UBSPD
UBS Publishers' Distributors Ltd.

UBS Publishers' Distributors Ltd.
5 Ansari Road, New Delhi-110 002
Bombay Bangalore Madras Calcutta Patna Kanpur London

First Published **1995**
First Reprint **1995**

Acknowledgements : M.J. Akbar/The Asian Age
Cover Design : UBS Art Studio
Cover Photographs : N.K. Sareen

Designed & Typeset at UBSPD in 11 pt Souvenir
Printed at Rajkamal Electric Press, New Delhi

To
the girl who matters more in my life
than any other man or woman
I have written about –
My grand-daughter
Naina Dayal

Contents

Introduction

Thousands of men and women come into the life of every person. A few relationships abide, most are short lived. In the first category are members of the family into which one is born: grandparents, parents, uncles, aunts, brothers and sisters, cousins and others who come into the family by marriage. In the second are others who come close to them in school or college days or later in their careers. Most of these associations are stronger because they are self-acquired and not inherited by accident of birth. However, they are also shorter in duration. In the beginning they can be intense like love between adolescents or adults. When the ardour begins to subside they begin to drift apart, make newer relationships which also run their course and come to an end. After a while they are completely forgotten. It is of some of these kinds of transient relationships that I have written about in this book. As a passage in *The Mahabharata* says they are like two planks of wood floating in the ocean. Waves bring them together side by side and make them appear inseparable. Then the same waves separate them till they lose sight of each other. Such relationships are items for one's autobiography. I have written about them in my life story to be published later this year.

I have chosen my subjects at random — mostly those men and women I befriended in my 60s and 70s. Some were offended with what I wrote about them and are no longer on talking terms with me; some pleased with the confession of affection I have made. And yet others, without bothering to read what I had written about them, said they don't give a damn about what I think of them. Now it is up to you to decide whether or not the exercise has been worthwhile.

— K.S.

Part One

WOMEN

Devyani Chaubal

Witty and malicious Devyani had no respect for the tinsel stars.

Dharmendra was known to be a bit of a stud; Devyani's account made him out to be a superstud. She wrote about how he serviced two to three starlets every day in the studios before he returned home to do his "home work" on his wife's bed. Dharmendra was understandably very upset. He waylaid her one afternoon near the race course.

I have very little interest, hence lesser knowledge of Hindi films and film stars. When persuaded to see one, I have rarely sat through it to the end. I find Hindi films too obvious, too contrived and absurd beyond belief. There are few actors and actresses whose talent I admire but find most of the others loud and unintelligent. I have never subscribed to a film journal and know next to nothing about the private lives of these tinsel stars.

When I first arrived in Bombay in 1969 to take over the editorship of *The Illustrated Weekly of India*, I found scores of film magazines delivered to me free of charge. I began to turn over their pages to see the photographs they published. The only texts I could bear to read were those written by Devyani Chaubal. They were witty and malicious and written in a *khichdi* of Hindi-English terminology I had not come across before. I was charmed by the way she threw in Hindustani words like *lafda, hangama, borobar, bhaav, bindaas, chaaloo, khalaas,* and scores of others in her narrative and dialogue. While going through her columns, I picked up a lot of spicy gossip about film personalities.

It was evident that Devyani had no respect for the men and women she wrote about. She mimicked their speech, mocked their pretensions and had a hearty laugh at their expense. I wanted to get to know her.

I wondered if she was any relation of Nalini Chaubal who had worked for me for a few days in London. Nalini was a frail, sallow-complexioned girl whose room had been burgled by a thug who thought she was a princess. All he got was a necklace made of glass beads.

When she came to see me she was in a state of shock. I persuaded High Commissioner Krishna Menon to give her a job as a clerk and asked her to move into my house for a few days. Soon after she returned to India and I lost track of her.

It was at a lunch party in a restaurant in Churchgate. There was a large crowd of mediapersons present. A tall, heavily built young woman came and introduced herself, "I am Nalini's younger sister, Devyani." She was a couple of inches taller than me, of more than ample girth, light-skinned and with curly dark brown hair. She had a beautiful face with full lips and long eyelashes curving up like scimitars. She was draped in a white sari with large floral patterns. Her voice was husky. I could hardly believe she could be the sister of the petite Nalini. We spent the lunch hour together and agreed to see more of each other.

Thereafter we met once almost every week. Her whereabouts always remained a mystery to me. She never told me where she lived, her telephone numbers were constantly changing.

She usually dropped in on me in the office and spent an hour gossiping away about the film world. She was a wonderful mimic and made film celebrities appear as silly as they were. She left me in splits of laughter.

It was sometime later that she agreed to see me in my apartment and she used to talk away while I was having my drink. She did not touch alcohol. I often took her out to dinner parties to which I was invited. Our hosts were always happy to receive her because she was quite a celebrity. On a couple of occasions she accompanied me to stag parties where blue films were shown.

She did not touch a drink and ate very little. She never let anyone drop her home and invariably took a taxi. Who her other male friends were I never got to know.

Devyani had more than her share of trouble writing the way she did of film personalities. Once she wrote about a male actor who had a short spell of success but was then on the decline. She prophesied that his days were over and a small mercy it was.

A few days later she went to a film party at Sun-n-Sand on Juhu beach. Not many guests were eager to talk to her, so she went out in the garden and sat down on a parapet overlooking the sea.

Two young men spotted her sitting alone and came lurching towards her. They were sons of the man she had denigrated in her column. Without warning they showered her with the filthiest of abuses. One boy emptied a bottle of beer on her head while the other continued to warn her what they would do to her fat behind the next time she wrote that kind of thing about their father. Devyani yelled "*bachao, bachao*", but no one came to her help. She had no friends.

She went to the police station and lodged an F.I.R. against the two boys. The next morning she came to my office to tell me about the incident. With tears streaming down her eyes she repeated over and over again what the boys had threatened to do to her, "We'll bugger you bloody bitch till your fat bum is blue; we will f... you till you scream for help", etc. I wasn't sure whether Devyani was really hurt or enjoying living through the experience by repeating the threats.

On another occasion she wrote a very bitchy piece on Dharmendra allegedly based on an interview he had given her. He was known to be a bit of a stud; Devyani's account made him out to be a superstud. She wrote about how he serviced two to three starlets every day in the studios before he returned home to do his "home work" on his wife's bed. Dharmendra was understandably very upset.

He waylaid her one afternoon near the race course. Devyani tried to run away, but with her bulk and floppy sari she could not get away from the athletic Dharmendra. He gave her the choicest Punjabi abuse and slapped her. Once again Devyani lodged an F.I.R. at the police station.

The news made the front pages of all the Bombay papers. Far from defending her I wrote in my column that if she had written the same kind of thing about me, I would have rewarded her the same way as did Dharmendra.

Dharmendra came to thank me; the police quashed the charge of assault of beating against him. I had to face a very angry and tearful Devyani. She let me have it.

Oddly enough this did not end our friendship. We continued to meet as before. She introduced me to many film stars. She took me to Raj Kapoor's home-theatre where we saw the opening scenes of *Satyam, Shivam, Sundaram* and dined with him and Zeenat Aman.

She was my passport to every film preview and film party. More than the previews and the parties I looked forward to Devyani's mimicry of the people we saw and met.

There are some women whose beauty lies in their bulk. Devyani was one of them. No sooner than they lose weight, they lose much of their charm. But Devyani was very self-conscious of her size and visibly upset when she overheard someone refer to her as *woh motee aurat*. Despite my pleadings and warnings she went on a crash course of dieting. She was never a big eater and she hardly took any exercise excepting rushing between her office to parties and cinema shows.

Depriving herself of the little food she ate did her no good. She did lose weight. But where there was firm flesh, now there were wrinkles. She also lost a lot of her lovely curls.

The last time I saw her in Bombay was at the Gymkhana Club. Before I could say anything she said, "You know how much weight I have shed? Look." She turned, pointing to her bare midriff. "All gone. And don't you tell me slimming down does not suit me."

I did not want to hurt her and so I remained quiet.

A few months later after I had returned to Delhi, I heard Devyani had been stricken with paralysis. One side of her was completely numb. She could no longer go about; her right side had ceased to function.

The Government of Maharashtra provided her with an apartment and domestic help. Devyani had to do her columns dictating them to a stenographer. I don't know how she manages to write about film people she no longer meets and about films she no longer sees.

I wrote her a long letter protesting my everlasting affection for her and asking her if there was anything I could do to be of assistance to her. After a month I got an answer. It was a typed letter—unsigned. She thanked me for my letter and offer of assistance. She did not need any. She is too proud to ask for help.

I have been to Bombay many times since but have not had the courage to call on her. I want to preserve the image of the Devyani Chaubal I had known: fat, full of life, malicious gossip, mimicry and zest for life.

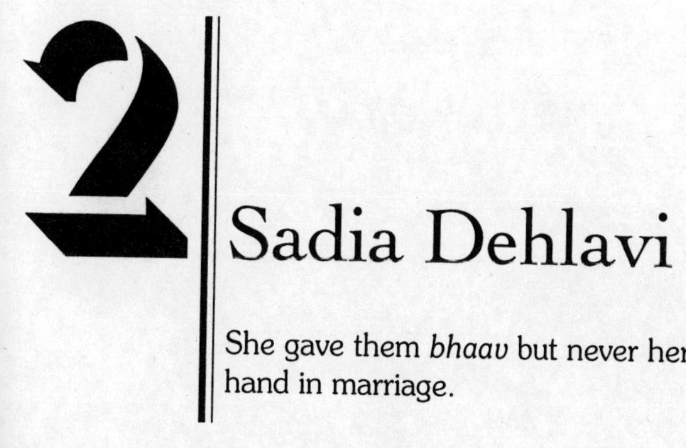

2 Sadia Dehlavi

She gave them *bhaav* but never her hand in marriage.

The 45-year difference in our ages did not make the slightest difference.... Although often seen with me, I meant to keep our friendship to ourselves. Not Sadia. She proclaimed from the house-tops and in interviews to Bombay's gossip magazines said, "the only man in my life is Khushwant Singh."

It was at an exhibition of Amina Ahuja's calligraphy that I first met her, in 1987. "Come, let me introduce you to Sadia Dehlavi," said Amina taking me by my hand and leading me to a girl sitting on a *moorha* in the middle of a crowded room. The girl didn't bother to get up. She simply gaped at me with her large, luscious eyes. Her jet-black hair cascaded in curls round her oval face. There was nothing I could think of saying to her except blurting out, "Why are you so beautiful?"

Her face flushed with joy as she put out her hand and replied: "If you think I am beautiful, I must be beautiful", or words to that effect. I had not caught her name and asked her to tell me again. "Sadia Dehlavi," she replied. "You must have heard of the Dehlavis of the *Shama* group of journals. I am Yunus Dehlavi's daughter. I edit an Urdu magazine *Bano*."

I spent an hour talking to her. I invited her to my home to meet my family. From that day to the time she married Reza Parvez and left for Pakistan, Sadia remained my closest friend. The 45-year difference in our ages did not make the slightest difference. Nor the fact that she came from a conservative Muslim family well-known in northern India and I, an aged Sikh, was often described by the gutter press as "the dirty old man of Delhi". Although often seen with me, I meant to keep our friendship to ourselves. Not Sadia. She proclaimed from the house-tops and in interviews to Bombay's gossip magazines said, "the only man in my life is Khushwant Singh".

Sadia was emotionally very promiscuous. And utterly outspoken. She talked to me by the hour telling me of the many men in her life. She had made disastrous marriage to the scion of a family which ran the leading Urdu daily in Calcutta. Her husband was mother-ridden and prone to violence. She divorced him and returned to her parents' home. She was a restless character, ever changing her jobs and admirers. She would open a boutique one day and talk of the millions she would make in a few months; close it after a few days to start a furniture business. Then take a franchise in a restaurant and give it up in a few days to make bigger millions by exporting carpets. For a while she toyed with the notion of getting into politics. She led a march to Meerut where communal riots had broken out and tried to nurse Jamia Nagar and Zakir Bagh which had sizeable Muslim populations as her constituency. She went abroad a few times. Once in England she ran out of money and worked as a barmaid in a pub serving beer to customers. To atone for her "sins", on her way back to India, she broke journey to perform an Umra pilgrimage at Mecca and Madina. She had a natural flair for writing and was commissioned by *India Today* as well as *The Times of India* to write regular columns for them. No one could have asked for a bigger break. Her enthusiasm lasted a few weeks. She quickly got bored with anything she did. At one time she took to riding; then decided to learn flying. She hired a *maulvi* sahib to teach her Persian and Arabic. Then the zest for living got the better of the desire to become a scholar. She loved animals and once bought a cuddly little cocker spaniel. One day she dumped it in the flat of her then closest girl friend, Kamna Prasad, promising to pick it up later that evening. Three days later Kamna had to deposit the pup in Sadia's home.

Sadia had a grasshopper's personality. Above everyone else she loved herself. Once she was in the press party which accompanied Rajiv Gandhi on a foreign tour. Being much the most photogenic in the group, next to the Prime Minister, she attracted more attention on TV and the media. For a while she toyed with the idea of joining the Congress party and getting into one or the other houses of Parliament, but soon got bored with the notion.

One thing Sadia was consistent about was wanting to get married. More than marriage, she wanted to be a mother. Her husband had to be a Muslim. The father of her child had to be Muslim. When the late Ismat Chugtai advised her to be bold and produce a bastard — *haraamee paida kar* — Sadia was appalled.

Many eligible men proposed marriage to her: she gave them *bhaav* but never her hand in marriage. Ultimately it was Reza Parvez, almost twenty years older than her, divorced father of two grown-up children and a Shia (Sadia is Sunni) who wore down Sadia's resistance. Her mother kept telling her to the last day of her marriage that if she wanted to change her mind, she could do so before signing the *nikahnamah*. She did not change her mind. I signed the *nikahnamah* as a witness to her consent to marry Reza. I thought Sadia would take Pakistani citizenship and go out of my life. Once again I had misjudged Sadia.

A few months after Sadia and Reza had settled down in Islamabad to what appeared to me blissful happy matrimony they came to meet me in Lahore where I had been invited to deliver the Manzur Qadir Memorial Lecture on Indo-Pak relations. Sadia came to the lecture dressed in a gorgeous sari: Pakistani women invariably wore *shalwar-kameez*. Sadia sported a red *bindi* on her forehead: in Pakistan this was the sign of *kufr* (heresy) worn by infidels. She had become aggressively Indian in a country which regarded India as enemy number one. In course of time a Pakistan rag denounced Sadia as an Indian spy. She became *persona non grata* in Pakistani society. Reza was fired from his job.

Sadia was confused and unhappy. Far from being a *Grahlakshmi*, she had brought misfortune on her husband's household. She was back in Delhi looking for a career and seeing gynaecologists to tell her why she had not conceived. Reza, she confided to me, was a great lover. The couple returned to Pakistan. Reza had to sell his house in Karachi to keep the home fires burning. Slowly the wheel of fortune turned in their favour. Reza found a job; Sadia was pregnant. A son was born to them. They named him Armaan. Six months later Sadia brought Armaan to meet his real grandfather – me. She chided me for not having dedicated any book to her. I did: *Not a Nice Man to Know* (Penguin/Viking) bears the dedication:

To Sadia Dehlavi
who gave me more affection and notoriety
than I deserved.

Indrani Aikath Gyaltsen

Hold My Hand, I Am Dying, she wrote.
But when she died there was no one with her.

Indrani and I talked into the late hours, occasionally holding hands. She must have smoked away a whole packet of cigarettes and I must have imbibed a few goblets of cognac. When we decided to call it a day, reluctantly, we were both a little giddy and drawn to each other.

Of all the women who came into my life, Indrani Aikath Gyaltsen's friendship with me was perhaps of the shortest duration. We met briefly with long breaks in between because she lived in Darjeeling, Calcutta and Chaibasa (Bihar), and I in Delhi. But we managed to span these long distances by writing to each other almost twice a week and frequently ringing each other up.

She came into my life through the good offices of the wife of the then German Ambassador who had stayed with her in the Glenburn tea estate, some 20 miles downhill from Darjeeling. The estate was managed by her Tibetan husband Sonam Gyaltsen. Indrani was keen on writing. Some of her articles had been published in Calcutta papers. She wanted to explore further avenues. "Could you help her?" asked Her Excellency.

I wrote to Indrani to send me some of her writings. She did, adding that she would be in Delhi for a couple of days and asked me if she could meet me. I invited her to dinner at the Meridien.

I left a word with the reception to send the lady who asked for me to the coffee shop. I took a seat from where I could see the reception desk. At that time I had no idea whether she was an Indian or a Tibetan. I did not know that Aikath was a Bengali Kayastha surname.

I saw a diminutive figure approach the clerk at the reception desk and he pointed towards the coffee shop. As she entered, I stood up to greet her.

She had no difficulty in spotting me: I was the only Sardar in the cafe. We shook hands and took our seats facing each other. And obviously take each other's measure. After asking her, I ordered two Scotch 'n' soda. While waiting for her drink, she lit a cigarette, a foreign brand, with a silver lighter. While she told me of her background I took a good look at her: light brown complexion, slightly puffed out cheeks, jet-black hair cropped short, eyebrows severely trimmed to appear like thin lines; heavy make-up; heavy aroma of French perfume; lots of jewellery: earrings, necklace, bracelets; altogether overdressed.

She had a soft gentle voice and spoke without any trace of a regional accent. She told me her father was a mine owner who had his home and fortune in Chaibasa. She had a younger sister, married and with children. She too had first married a Bengali in the IAS, found him a bore, divorced him and then married Sonam. They had a son Siddharttha in school in Darjeeling.

"I could have married a Sardar after I divorced my first husband. He was then a brigadier. He is now a full general," she told me. "Why didn't you?" I asked her. "Did you find out just in time that many Sardar husbands are wife-beaters?" She laughed, "No, it was much worse. He spoke English with a Punjabi accent. How could I live the rest of my life with a man who mispronounced every word he spoke?"

When dinner was served we turned to the topic of writing as a career. She told me she had written lots of poetry. "There is no money in poetry. Most poetry published in India is at the poet's expense. Professor P. Lal's Writers' Workshop does that kind of thing. Neither reviewers nor booksellers touch them because there are no buyers," I told her.

"Does that mean you don't want to see my poetry?" she asked.

"Not at all! By all means send it to me. But I don't know the first thing about modern poetry. I only read established poets. Full stop with T.S. Eliot."

A few months later she sent me a collection of her poems published by none other than Writers' Workshop. I could not come to terms with her poems and even the dedication did not make sense: it was dedicated to me. She seemed too easy a conquest.

A year passed. My wife and I happened to visit Bhutan. Indrani asked us to make a small detour and be her guests in Darjeeling. I had never seen that part of the country and agreed to do so. After a long drive through miles of tea estates we arrived in time at the planters' club for lunch. Indrani was very excited and introduced me to her husband, a very handsome man, and to all her tea planter friends, mainly Punjabis with fat, bejewelled wives.

It was a tortuous drive downhill to Glenburn. It was a spacious well-kept bungalow done up in upper class European style. Not a touch of *desi* about anything: Crockery, cutlery, decanters, cut-glass tumblers. My wife was tired after the long journey from Thimpu and retired to bed. So did Sonam who had a heavy day ahead of him. Indrani and I talked into the late hours occasionally holding hands. She must have smoked away a whole packet of cigarettes and I must have imbibed a few goblets of cognac. When we decided to call it a day, reluctantly, we were both a little giddy and drawn to each other. A good night kiss was not out of place.

The next day we left for Delhi. Our correspondence became more frequent and informal. Gradually Indrani drew me into her domestic problems. She was bored being the wife of a tea planter with little to do except entertain other tea planters and businessmen. Sonam was a nice, considerate husband with no other interests except tea and not very communicative. Could I help her son get admission to a good college? Could I help her sort out the mess created by her ageing father in his mining business?

I did whatever she wanted me to: write to vice-chancellors and principals of colleges, ministers, chief ministers and take her to meet officials whenever she came to Delhi.

My nagging her bore fruit. She sent me the manuscript of her first novel: *Daughters of the House*. She had made me read the first three chapters several times.

I passed on the complete novel to my wife. She was most impressed. Then I passed it on to David Davidar of Penguin-Viking. He too was taken up by it and issued her a contract. It got excellent reviews and was accepted by foreign publishers.

"I can turn out that kind of novel every six months," she told David. "Do so," he replied. "I will commission you to write ten novels."

I thought Indrani was riding on cloud nine. But she was impatient for fame and money. We met at the Calcutta book fair. Her second novel *Crane's Morning* was due to be released that week. "Why don't people ask me for autographs? Why am I not as widely read as Shobha Dé?" She asked me. I assured her that after she had published a few more novels, people would seek her out. And as for selling like Shobha Dé, I told her, "Put some fucking in your writing and you will be as widely read." She did not approve of my language. "I am not that kind of a writer," she replied with haughty disdain.

Indrani moved from Darjeeling to Calcutta where her husband had an apartment. Then to Chaibasa to look after her father who had suffered a stroke and was paralysed on one side. I had not met her for many months and was eager to be with her. I accepted an invitation to speak at Ranchi which is barely an hour's drive from Chaibasa. Indrani was at Ranchi airport to receive me. She had booked a room in the same hotel and apart from my engagements, we spent the rest of the time together. I made an appointment with Dr. N.K. Sinha, the leading doctor in Ranchi, to give an opinion on Indrani's father. She had brought his medical reports with her. He examined the X-ray reports and told her candidly: "I don't give him more than a few months." (He died three months later.)

After meeting the doctor we did the countryside of Ranchi: the hilltop house where Rabindranath Tagore and his brother had lived for a few months; some ancient temples and even lunatic asylums. My age and faltering steps gave me the excuse to hold her hand or rest mine on her shoulder. It was a most pleasant sensation.

Crane's Morning did better than her first novel. This book was also dedicated to me. She was commissioned by *The Statesman* to write a weekly column for it. She was very excited. At long last Calcutta society would get to know her name.

Despite the success that came to her, Indrani was very unsure of herself. She spent a week with us in Delhi. Every afternoon she went to Khan Market and spent thousands of rupees buying new dresses and jewellery. "When you want to give me an expensive present buy me expensive gold earrings," she said. And every other evening when we were alone she would suddenly turn around and ask me: "Khushwant, do you think I am beautiful?"

Indrani's meteoric decline began in early 1993. I could sense it coming. She began to take her *Statesman* assignment very casually and simply churned out whatever came to her mind. They refused to publish some pieces as she sent them and then cancelled her contract. She asked me to speak to the editor. I refused. "You asked for it," I told her. "Column writing is not as easy as most people think."

For reasons unknown to me, instead of staying on in Calcutta or joining her husband in Darjeeling, Indrani returned to Chaibasa to live with her widowed mother and sister with whom she was barely on talking terms. She worked on her third novel, and as usual, sent me each chapter as she finished them. I wrote to her, asking her to send me the complete manuscript. Without reading it I passed it on to David. He accepted it but asked her to change the title. I could not understand why her letters started getting shorter and shorter. She complained of being depressed all the time. I wrote back to say that no one except herself could help her overcome her depression. Her last letter to me was barely two paragraphs. She wrote: "You are right, no one can help me except myself. I do not have the will to live. I do not have the will to die." A day before the letter reached me, Sonam rang up from Chaibasa to say that Indrani was dead.

Was it suicide? Later events lend credence to the version that she might have taken her own life. A publisher sent a legal notice to Penguin-Viking claiming that several pages in *Crane's Morning* had been lifted from a novel *The Rosemary Tree* published by them over 20 years earlier.

It is more than likely that some readers might have written to her accusing her of plagiarism and she realised it would soon be known to everyone. She could not face the world being charged with that kind of misdemeanour. It is ironic that her last novel is titled: *Hold My Hand, I Am Dying*. She died alone with no one to hold her hand.

Once I told her that the last book I would do is an anthology of my favourite love poetry in English, Urdu, Hindi and Punjabi. "Will you dedicate it to me?" she asked.

I promised to do so. I also have an enlarged colour photograph of Indrani Aikath Gyaltsen in my study in Kasauli.

Ghayoorunnissa Hafeez

The girl in a *burqa* who changed forever my attitude towards Muslims.

Her parting words brought tears to my eyes. "I have no one left in the world who bothers about me except you.... My parents and all my sisters are dead. Why does not Allah listen to my prayers and send for me. I don't want to live any longer."

Ghayoorunnissa Hafeez of Hyderabad came into my life when I was seventeen years old. She was a couple of years older and had come to Delhi to join Lady Hardinge Medical College where her elder sister was studying.

After a year of medical studies she joined Lady Irwin College to take a degree in home science. My younger sister was a student there. The two girls became friends. She was invited to our home for a weekend.

She came draped in a *burqa*. At my sister's insistence she took it off and was introduced to the family. For me it was a bewitching experience: The art of unveiling is a dramatic event as spectacular as when a curtain goes up in a theatre revealing a stage brightly lit with coloured lights, resembling a fairyland.

My first impression was that she was beautiful beyond compare. Actually she was a small, frail girl with a sallow complexion and curly light brown hair. She spoke English without any regional accent: Her Urdu was delightfully *Dakhhani*. What really bowled me over was that a girl who had spent so many of her adolescent years in seclusion could be so saucy and forward.

A few days after she came to our home for the first time, my sister and I took her to the pictures. I sat between the two girls. No sooner were the lights dimmed, she took my hand under the folds of her sari. I was wild with joy. Thereafter I didn't have to bother with my sister.

Once she got permission to spend an evening at our home. I went to pick her up and instead of taking her home, I took her for a long drive round New Delhi. At that time it was still sparsely populated and the ridge was a welcome wilderness. We never got beyond holding hands and exchanging words of affection. She was very firm about how far unmarried people could go in getting to know each other.

We wrote long letters to each other. We continued writing to each other in the years I was in England. Her letters got shorter and rarer and then stopped altogether. I learnt from my sister that Ghayoor had got married to a Muslim army officer who also belonged to Hyderabad.

Why I regard my brief and near-platonic relationship with Ghayoor an important landmark in my life is that she changed my attitude towards Muslims.

Like other Hindus and Sikhs of my generation, I had been brought up on anti-Muslim prejudices based on Muslim stereotypes.

The first jolt came with my close association with the saintly *maulvi* Shafiuddin Nayyar, my Urdu teacher. A more upright and God-fearing man I had not met in my childhood.

Then came Ghayoorunnissa Hafeez who proved to me that members of the two communities could love each other. Once you fell in love with someone of another community, you fall in love with all her people. And finally there was Manzur Qadir. Everafter knowing these people I came to the naïve conclusion that an Indian Muslim could do no wrong.

Ghayoorunnissa resurfaced in my life 30 years later. My sister asked me over for breakfast at my parents' home. When I arrived there she asked me, "Do you recognise this girl?" Of course! It was Ghayoor. She was no longer a girl but a middle-aged woman who had buried two husbands. With her was a comely teenager, Fareesa, her daughter from her first husband. Fareesa joined Lady Irwin College. I was appointed her local guardian. Fareesa was very popular with college boys. Whenever she went out with them she left a note that she was going to see her local guardian. She had no problem extracting a letter from me saying she had spent the evening in my home.

Fareesa spent her first honeymoon with her English husband at my house. She divorced him and married a Swedish banker. They live in style in Hong Kong. Whenever I am in Hong Kong I stay with her. To her children from her two husbands, I am *nana* — maternal grandfather.

Once having re-established contact with Ghayoor, I never lost it. Every time I go to Hyderabad, we spend our evenings together. She has become very frail and nearly blind. She has also become very religious. It is five prayers a day and a daily appeal to Allah to send for her. The last time I was in Hyderabad, I had to track her down to an old ladies' home.

She took me to a *dargah* where her parents and sisters are buried. She has reserved a site for her own grave. "I paid Rs 1,500 for it 15 years ago. Today this would cost more than Rs 15,000," she told me. "Why don't you sell it and make a profit out of your own grave," I said trying to cheer her up. She turned down the suggestion.

"I have had salt sprinkled on the grave. It is a Hyderabadi custom. No one else besides me can be buried here."

Her parting words brought tears to my eyes. "I have no one left in the world who bothers about me except you. Fareesa is involved with her own family and hardly ever writes to me. My parents and all my sisters are dead. Why does not Allah listen to my prayers and send for me. I don't want to live any longer."

5

Anees Jung

I am tempted to write a novel with
Anees as the main character.

She could flatter any man out of his wits, then run him down while talking to others. And if confronted, flatly deny having done so... she is an incorrigible name-dropper, but the amazing truth is that she does in fact know all the names she drops.

If I had to draw a list of the most engaging conversationalists I have met in my life, the name of Anees Jung would come on top. That, despite the fact that I was never sure whether what she told me was true or a figment of her fantasies.

She could flatter any man out of his wits, then run him down while talking to others. And if confronted, flatly deny having done so. She does it to me all the time and yet I look forward to being with her. She is a good hostess, serves gourmet food and vintage wines. She often has well-known singers to entertain her guests. She is an incorrigible name-dropper, but the amazing truth is that she does in fact know all the names she drops.

To her home come Presidents of the Republic (Giani Zail Singh), cabinet ministers (Balram Jakhar, Ram Niwas Mirdha), leaders of the Opposition (Atal Behari Vajpayee), Governors (B.K. Nehru, L.K. Jha), national figures like Sheikh Mohammad Abdullah, poets like Ahmed Faraz, writers like V.S. Naipaul, ambassadors, counsellors — you name them, she knows them and they know her.

The paradigm in her scale of human being was what she describes as the "Renaissance gentleman": Well-dressed, sophisticated, *au courant* with the arts, literature and style of living. Her self-image is that of a Renaissance lady who gathers men around her. Where did I fit in her scheme of things?

Chronologically, I was the first to pick her up and give her a job. I have known her for over 30 years. And though often exasperated by her go-getting and saying nasty things about people behind their backs, I could never shed her. She took good care that I did not do so.

Sometime in the early 1960s, she returned with a degree from some American university. She rang up my wife to say that she had met our son in Bombay and he had suggested that she get in touch with his parents when she was in Delhi. She was promptly invited for lunch. Both of us were charmed by her. She bore an aristocratic, Hyderabadi name, Jung.

She spoke English without a trace of an American accent and Hindustani in the *Dakhani* lilt and mix-up of genders which I find very attractive. She was looking for a job. I had one, a temporary one, to offer. I was conducting a party of American students round the world. Two months were to be spent in India. We had done one month in Delhi. The second was to be in Hyderabad. The boys and girls had to be housed with Hyderabadi families and lectures arranged for them.

Anees was a Hyderabadi who knew the best families in the city. She accepted the job at what was then a handsome remuneration for one month. She executed her assignment with dispatch and found excellent homes for all my students and top academics like Professor Rashiduddin, MP, to speak to them. At the same time, instead of one Delhi-Hyderabad-Delhi air trip, she made me pay for three. She got under the skin of the family she was staying with and was unceremoniously thrown out on the road. Far from being crushed, she bounced back to life and made her presence felt in the city.

Whenever she came to see me in any hotel she drove up in the American Consul-General's big limousine. At a dinner reception given by this diplomat she overshadowed all the others present. Many guests got the impression she was closely connected with the royal family of the Nizam of Hyderabad.

Actually Anees Jung's ancestors were not from Hyderabad but from Lucknow. Her father, Hoshiar (a very apt name), migrated to Hyderabad and soon attracted the Nizam's attention. He was a very cultivated man with a gift for words. Though never formally given an official position, he was given a title, Nawab Hoshiar Jung, and became a very close companion *masahib* of His Exalted Highness and was granted a large *haveli* and other real estate in the city.

The family lived in feudal splendour till, for reasons unknown, he fell out of favour and lost most of what he had. Nothing now remains of Nawab Hoshiar Jung's wealth. However, Anees can be forgiven for believing that her father was a Minister (even Prime Minister) of Hyderabad.

Go-getting is Anees's second nature. Once when I was invited to Guwahati, a Canadian woman, Sue Dexter (over six feet tall), who wanted to see as much of India as she could in a fortnight, asked me if she could come along with me. I agreed that she could but warned her that I had many engagements in Guwahati and would not have much time to take her around. Also that she would have to find her own accommodation as I would be staying in the Circuit House.

She asked Anees, whose sister she knew, to come along as her escort. All expenses paid. We arrived at Guwahati to a guard of honour presented by the Khalsa High School and a band playing the national anthem. The two girls came to the Circuit House with me. Sue Dexter found a room in a small hotel. Anees rang up the Governor, B.K. Nehru, and told him she was a friend of his son and did not know where to stay in Guwahati. She was invited to stay at the Raj Bhawan.

For the next three days, the three of us rode in the Governor's car to see the sights along the Brahmaputra.

Her muscling in on President Zail Singh's visit to Bombay to inspect the Indian Navy was even more audacious. When I told her I had been invited by Gianiji, to accompany him, she simply rang up Rashtrapati Bhawan and told the President's secretary that she would be coming along as well.

We flew in the President's private plane. While I stayed in a hotel Anees was a guest of Governor Ali Yavar Jung. She flew back on the same plane. President Zail Singh was enchanted by her *bada gharana* upbringing and impeccable manners. Every Eid, a Presidential hamper of fruit was delivered at her flat.

I had many opportunities of seeing Anees Jung when I was editing *The Illustrated Weekly of India*. The board of Bennett Coleman wanted to launch a magazine for the young. I was involved with the choice of the editor. I chose Anees Jung. *Youth Times* was based in Delhi. But within a few weeks Anees had become a great favourite of the board, particularly the general manager, Mr. Ram Tarneja.

She was in and out of Bombay whenever she wished. Every evening she would be seen sitting in the back of Tarneja's car parked in the portico. All the staff going home saw her as the most privileged of editors of the *Times of India* group of papers.

I was very put off and decided to have nothing to do with her. For a couple of years after being thrown out of *The Illustrated Weekly of India* I refused to speak to her. At a reception in the house of the Pakistan High Commissioner, she came to sit near me. I got up and took another seat. "So it is still like that," she remarked and went into a sulk.

The *Youth Times* didn't last long. Anees was once again out of a job. Then for the first time she thought of doing some serious writing. Everyone was surprised to find she had a talent for good, straight and very evocative writing. I don't recall how we got together again, but she was with me when I went to Amritsar in June 1984 to see the havoc wrought by the Indian Army in Operation Bluestar. It was not I, a Sikh, but Anees Jung a Shia Muslim, who kept making offerings of flowers, money and *persaad* at every shrine we visited. She does not have an ounce of religious prejudice in her.

It would be unfair to describe Anees Jung as a *matlabee*, a seeker of favours. Her columns in *The Times of India* gave her an all-India readership. Her books were published by Penguin-Viking, notably *Unveiling India* went into many editions and opened many doors to her. She got a lucrative assignment from the UN to do a definitive book on the status of women in Asia. It was released at the UN conference on population in Cairo. She is currently with UNESCO in Paris to put forward the point of view of Asian women.

Anees Jung's books will be read by future generations and her name kept alive long after she is gone. All I can say is that I haven't met another woman quite like her. I am tempted to write a novel with Anees Jung as its main character.

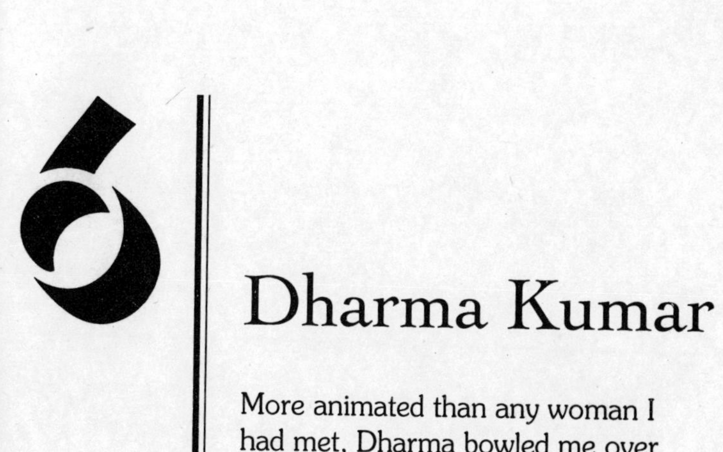

Dharma Kumar

More animated than any woman I
had met, Dharma bowled me over.

Undaunted by her indifference (and almost contempt), I continued to admire Dharma. When abroad, I wrote to her — long letters full of lyrical prose. Her replies were always short and very prosaic. At the height of my infatuation with her I dedicated my second novel to her.

Over 30 years ago at some lunch party in someone's garden I met Dharma Kumar and her husband Lavraj Kumar. He was a senior executive in Burmah Shell; she working on a doctoral thesis in Cambridge University. She was the centre of attraction.

She was more animated than any woman I had met: her eyes sparkled; her toes twitched; her hands were restless. She was an excellent mimic and delightfully malicious. I was completely bowled over. For the next few days I talked about her all the time and got as much detail of her past as I could get from people who knew her.

Lavraj was a UP Bania from a well-known family. He had won a Rhodes scholarship and got a degree from Oxford. She was a South Indian Brahmin, the only child of a distinguished scientist Dr. Venkatraman, head of the National Chemical Laboratory in Pune.

How and where the two had met and decided to get married I was not able to find out. It was from their friends I gathered that Dharma had a vastly exaggerated respect for academic achievements. To make her grade, one had to have a first class from a prestigious university. Most of her relations and men she admired had firsts from Oxford and Cambridge and went on to become civil servants or professors.

Lavraj had more than made the grade being a Rhodes scholar. What she could not make terms with was that he had opted to become a box-wallah in a firm till then dominated by Englishmen. Lavraj was a great favourite of the Bara Sahib Sinbad Sinclair and his rather bossy wife Eleanor. Dharma went out of her way to be rude to them.

The Sinclairs were one couple we shared in common. Eleanor was my closest English friend. I had once stayed with her in her Burmah Shell mansion overlooking the sea in Bombay and treated her home in Albion Street in central London as my own. I got on very well with her husband and children as well. I enjoyed being bossed over by Eleanor. Neither Dharma nor my wife had much patience with her.

I did not have the curriculum vitae to gain entrance to Dharma's charmed circle of friends. I had a very poor academic record, had done lowly jobs and the few books I had written were not highly rated in academic circles.

Oddly enough Dharma was also not the kind of woman I usually fell for. Although I was taken up by her looks she had no distinguishing features nor an hour-glass figure. She wore no make-up or perfume. It was her liveliness that I found irresistible. She was restless: her legs and hands were never still. She was not interested in animals and averse to physical contact with men. Come to think of it, the only reason she responded to my overtures was that I overwhelmed her with admiration. It was an entirely one-sided affair.

We began to invite the Lavraj Kumars to our small parties. Dharma was always the centre of attraction; her quiet, gentle self-effacing husband became the greater favourite with my wife and daughter. For the next few winters the Kumars and their daughter, Radha, became members of our small group which used to set out every Sunday morning before dawn, drive out of Delhi 20-30 miles to explore the countryside.

This group usually consisted of Evan Charlton (editor of *The Statesman*) and his wife Joy and their daughter Victoria, Herry Croom-Johnson (head of the British Council), and his wife Jane and Prem Kirpal. The most important member of the group was our German Shepherd Simba who was always in a high state of excitement to get out in the open country, chase rabbits, peacocks, or herds of cows. We would have our coffee and our sandwiches before we set out through rough country and agricultural fields ending on the banks of Jamuna.

After 2-3 hours of marathon walking, we returned to our base to drink chilled beer. These winter Sunday morning walks were most exhilarating. I made it a point to be with Dharma. She was obsessed with economics; I discovered that people she admired most were economists. I knew nothing about one or the other.

Undaunted by her indifference (and almost contempt), I continued to admire Dharma. When abroad, I wrote to her — long letters full of lyrical prose. Her replies were always short and very prosaic. At the height of my infatuation with her I dedicated my second novel *I Shall Not Hear the*

Nightingale to her. The dedication which was taken from lines of the poet Robert Browning read:

Paracelsus: ".... I am that aspired to know; and thou?"
Aprile: I would love infinitely and be loved.

To Dharma who aspires to know.

She was embarrassed by this public declaration of my feeling for her. I don't think she bothered to read the novel — or for that matter anything else I wrote. She treated me as a very light-weight character — which I no doubt was.

The break came very unexpectedly over a trivial incident. We were dining with the Lavraj Kumars. Dharma had got some kind of lecturing assignment abroad. She had special venom against fake academics who managed to get invitations from foreign universities and had nothing to show for them.

She casually told me that she was being invited by some British (or perhaps American) institution. Very light-heartedly, I remarked, "And how did you wangle it?" She went pale with anger and burst out, "I don't like that kind of insinuation. I am not a wangler."

The outburst of anger took me and all others at the dining table unawares. An uneasy silence descended on the tale. The party was ruined.

The one thing I could never forget or forgive is people losing their temper with me. I froze and swore to have nothing more to do with Dharma.

I did not ring her up as I used to. I did not invite her to join our Sunday morning walks. I think she sensed that I had been upset by her outburst of temper. But she was too proud to say sorry. She was unhappy that she had lost a devoted admirer and sent a common friend Ramu whom she admired very much to talk to me. He dropped in uninvited one evening to have a drink. In his own gentle way he conveyed to me that Dharma was unhappy that I had suddenly dropped her. I made no comments.

It was after many months later that we started seeing each other again. But it was never the same thing. Something in me had snapped and could not be rejoined. I felt more at ease with Lavraj and their daughter Radha than I did with Dharma.

We resumed asking each other to our homes for meals, but I was always on my guard lest I say something that may trigger off another explosion of ill-temper. When her mother died in Delhi after a long illness, I wrote to her and we went to condole with her.

At the time Lavraj had left Burmah Shell and joined government service as secretary of the Petroleum Ministry. He was now much more the kind of man whose wife Dharma would have liked to be. They were allotted a large bungalow on Willingdon Crescent with a three-acre garden.

Lavraj was able to indulge in his passion for growing exotic vegetables like broccoli, Brussels, sprouts and asparagus. Whenever we called on them, they gave us the produce of their garden.

Dharma was never one to entertain her husband's bosses or ministers of government. Her paradigm remained bright academics. Her parties continued to be made round some eminent visiting professor or the other. She tried to make her chief guest by inviting Indians of matching ability. Amongst her favourites were L.K. Jha, Professor K.N. Raj and Ramaswamy.

Despite her indifference towards people in power, she took good care to provide excellent food. I don't think she bothered to go into her kitchen but always employed good cooks. Though her husband was secretary of an important ministry and possessed considerable inherited wealth (Lavraj was like Dharma the only child of his parents), he could not ensure a regular supply of Scotch.

When inviting me for a meal Dharma, knowing how fussy I was about what I drank, would word her invitation aggressively. "K. Singh you and Sardarni come for dinner. I am sorry I have no Scotch. Frankly I don't care. You'll have to do with what we have."

To anyone else I would have said "No thank you" or "Can I bring my own Scotch?" But with Dharma I could no longer take such liberties. I took the Indian whisky Lavraj poured out and said, "If you had not told me that it was Indian I wouldn't have known." It was not true.

Lavraj retired from government service and had to vacate his large bungalow on Willingdon Crescent. He had a nice apartment of his own in Sunder Nagar which he had rented out to someone who had promised to vacate it as soon as he was asked to do so. It took Lavraj ten years to get the fellow out.

We were invited over when the flat was still being renovated. There was no Sctoch but Dharma bubbled with vitality as ever she did. Radha had not done as well as they had hoped and was living on her own. Dharma had reconciled herself to her daughter living her own life. So reluctantly had Lavraj. Both were touchy about outsiders commenting on their daughter's career. I had become very fond of Radha but did not dare say anything about her. The fear of provoking Dharma's anger persisted.

A few months ago, one morning, someone rang me up to say Lavraj had been rushed to Escorts Hospital and was in the intensive care unit. A few minutes later the same person rang up to say Lavraj had succumbed to a massive heart attack. The funeral would take place that afternoon.

There was a large turn-out at the electric crematorium. As I embraced Radha, I broke down in tears. It was Radha who consoled me. I looked round in the crowd for Dharma. Lavraj's uncle Dharmvira told me she had not come.

She could not take any public display of sorrow: mourning for her was a strictly personal and private affair. Thereafter whenever we met we promised to ask each other over for a meal. But neither of us has done so.

Nirmala Matthan

The people around took us to be father and daughter together on a pilgrimage. I felt relaxed and fulfilled...

I was already on cloud nine when one of Nirmala's friends came and announced in the hearing of all her family, "You look like a very happily married couple." Nirmala blushed with embarrassment. I protested, "She is younger than my daughter. How can you say such a thing!" The lady persisted, "Never mind the age difference, you still look like a married couple."

I cannot recall when and where I first met Nirmala Matthan. It was probably at some party in Bombay in the early 1970s. I had often seen her on Doordarshan (Indian TV) reading the news or some commentary. She was very photogenic and had a near-husky voice very soothing to the ear.

I was commissioned by the Guru Gobind Singh Foundation to make discs on the origin and development of

Sikhism to mark the Guru's 300th birth anniversary. I wrote the script and asked Nirmala to be the main voice reading the translations of passages from the Gurbani that I had incorporated in the script.

For about a fortnight we spent our mornings in the recording studios reading prose passages and filming them with *keertan* sung by Sindhi ladies and Sikh *raagis*.

Four discs were made by Polydor and put in the market under the title "Sikhism through the Songs of the Gurus". The Foundation President Sardar Ujjal Singh, then Governor of Tamil Nadu, was very pleased with them. Apart from the satisfaction it gave me to project the faith in which I was born, I earned the friendship of Nirmala Matthan.

What came as a pleasant surprise to me was that though Nirmala was a devout Syrian Christian she put so much of her soul into reading passages from the Gurbani. It was not a mechanical, professional performance but something in which she had put in all her emotions.

We started meeting occasionally for lunch. At times she came to my flat to have a drink with me. I confess I found her somewhat heavy going as she said very little besides answering my questions. And though I found her very attractive: dark, beautifully shaped and lustrous-eyed, she was also very straight-laced. It was after many meetings that I was able to piece together fragments of her past life.

Nirmala is one of the four children of General and Mrs P.T. Joseph. Her father, to whom she was devoted, was in the Indian Medical Service. Nirmala was born in Trivandrum but hardly ever lived there.

The family moved from one cantonment to another where her father was posted: Kohat, Rawalpindi, Pune, Deolali, Agra, and finally Delhi. So, Nirmala went to nine different schools before she joined Jesus and Mary Convent in Delhi and did her Senior Cambridge. She went on to Miranda House to take an honours degree in English literature. She also got a diploma in French and topped the list in Delhi University.

Music and theatre were Nirmala's abiding passions since her childhood. She sang in the church choir and on the stage; she also played the violin. The one time I was invited to dine with the family, I saw a piano in the sitting room.

Nirmala's career was dictated by her twin passions. She went for audition to All India Radio. Melville deMello, then the doyen of the broadcasting community, told her, "You are a born broadcaster."

She continued to sing, act, and compere programmes in Delhi till her parents came up with a marriage proposal for her.

Balu Matthan was a young engineer working with a large Marwari concern in Bombay. Needless to add, he was a Syrian Christian earning a good salary, and had a flat of his own. They got married.

To this day Nirmala has not divulged her date of birth or year of marriage to me. She is vain about her looks as she has every reason to be (Behram Contractor — Busy Bee — listed her among the five most beautiful women he had known). She looks much younger than anyone would think.

I have calculated her age from those of her two children, her son Uday, her daughter Poornima, and from a slip of the tongue admitting she had been married for over thirty years.

She must be in her early fifties; she looks like her daughter's elder sister. I have carefully looked to find out if she dyes her hair. I have not detected a single wisp of grey on her head.

When I left Bombay to return to Delhi, Nirmala gave me a large photograph of herself to take with me. Once when she came to Delhi, I invited her over for lunch.

That morning I put her photograph under the glass top of my working table in my study. I took her to my study to show it to her as an example of my undying affection for her.

"See, Nirmala, where I keep you?" I said. She saw through the ruse. "You are a liar?" she said. "You put it there this morning. You can't fool me so easily."

We kept up spasmodic correspondence. She wrote to me to say she was going to Kerala as her father was very ill. I rang her up wherever she was (Trivandrum or Cochin) to find out how he was. He died a few days later. Nirmala was devastated. And more hurt that the passing of a man who had risen so high in service and spent his days of retirement running a free clinic for the poor had barely been noticed by the media. There were a few lines about him in the local papers.

I asked her to send me his photograph and biodata. I paid General Joseph a handsome tribute in my column. With Nirmala it was (and is) a simple formula: She gladly gives her affection to anyone who says nice things about her father.

Whenever I went to Bombay I made it a point to ask Nirmala for a meal. As I said, she was an awkward guest to have as she hardly said anything herself besides replying to my stream of questions. When I ran out of something new to ask, the silence could be oppressive.

I discovered that the one thing that turned Nirmala on was music, Western classical as well as pop. She made an excellent compere for Hindustani classical music as well. Every time I travelled abroad by Air India and plugged in the earphones, it was Nirmala's recorded voice telling me what I was going to hear. It gave me a strange sort of feeling of closeness. I bought Western classical music tapes for her and gave her my books. I believe in bribing women to keep their affections.

The last time I was in Bombay, staying at the Sea Rock Hotel, I asked Nirmala over for drinks and dinner. I had run out of questions I could put to her and was apprehensive about how the evening would go. It was a memorable success without my having to keep the conversation going.

We went into the hotel restaurant specialising in seafood. It was empty. A Goan violinist was playing old tunes with no one to listen to him. He came to our table and asked us if there was anything special we would like to hear.

I could only think of tunes of bygone days: *Red sails in the sunset*, *One day my prince will come*, etc. He played them: Nirmala opened up with her full-throated voice and sang with him. People from the neighbouring room started filing in. Soon the seafood restaurant was full.

The general manager sent his photographer to take a picture of the violinist and Nirmala and sent drinks for us on the house. It was a roaring success.

After her husband's retirement from service, the Matthans moved to Bangalore where they owned an ancestral home in Richmond Town. As in Bombay so in Bangalore, whenever I went there I asked Nirmala over to have lunch or tea with me.

One Sunday she asked me if I would like to accompany the family to the mid-morning service in the cathedral. I readily agreed. I hadn't been to church since Nirmala had taken me to one in Bombay where she was singing. It was at this morning service where a number of young boys and girls were to be confirmed that I discovered that not only Nirmala, but also her husband, son and daughter were equally fond of singing. Thereafter I began referring to them as the singing Matthans.

The only member of the family who was unmusical was their fluffy little dog named Aristotle (Ari for short). He made up by sitting in everyone's lap in turns and licking their faces.

Both Nirmala's children work for ad agencies. At the annual Big Bang of the Bangalore Advertising Club where I was invited to give away the prizes, I saw the Matthans in full form. Most of the background singing was rendered by Uday and Poornima. They made the evening for the advertising fraternity.

It was a long affair. I was very tired and my throat was parched. Nirmala realised that I had had enough for my age and took me by the hand to sit on a sofa in the corner of the banqueting hall. Soon we became the centre of attention, surrounded by photographers and Nirmala's admirers. Her husband Balu stood away to let us bask in the glow of admiration. I had more than one frothing tankard of chilled lager followed by slugs of Scotch. I don't know who paid for them.

I was already on cloud nine when one of Nirmala's friends came and announced in the hearing of all her family, "You look like a very happily married couple". Nirmala blushed with embarrassment. I protested, "She is younger than my daughter. How can you say such a thing!"

The lady persisted, "Never mind the age difference, you still look like a married couple." I slipped out of the dining hall and went to bed without dinner. After the compliment I didn't need any. I was a little worried about how the rest of Nirmala's family would take that *faux pas*.

It did not bother them. We resumed our correspondence as if nothing had been said.

Last July I was in Bangalore again. It was a Sunday. I rang up Nirmala as soon as I was in my room and asked her to come over after the church service was over. "I am not going to church this Sunday. I can come over whenever you are free." She came for tea.

The next two days whenever I was free she came over and joined me in excursions to places in Bangalore I had not seen before. We visited two cave temples.

I hesitated to drink any of the *amrit* that was poured in my palm (for reasons of hygiene). The devout Syrian Christian Nirmala gulped it down with reverence, daubed her face with aromatic smoke and took the *prasad* of half a banana and half a coconut to eat at home.

In the dark, cavernous temple the floor was uneven and slippery because of coagulated coconut juice, and Nirmala firmly held my hand as a loving daughter would that of an ageing sire unsteady on his feet. The people around took us to be father and daughter together on a pilgrimage. I was full of gratitude, relaxed and fulfilled.

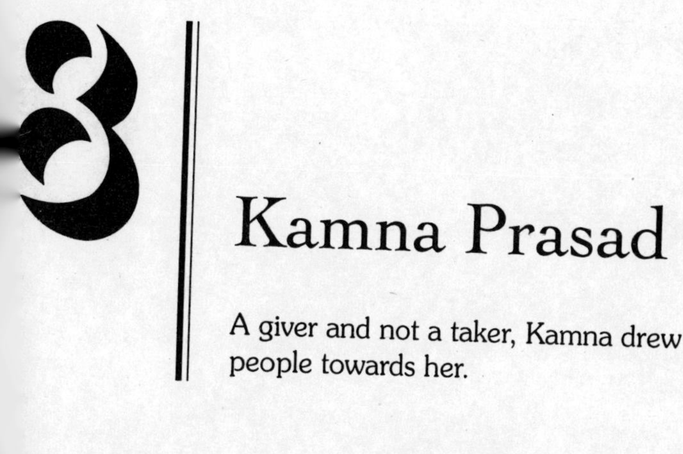

3 Kamna Prasad

A giver and not a taker, Kamna drew people towards her.

She was drawn towards the painter M.F. Hussain and enjoyed the attention he paid her.... Then he started to take her for granted. She gave him a short shrift and refused to talk to him. Hussain pleaded with me to beg her to forgive him. She did at her own terms.

It was sometime in 1980 soon after I had taken over the editorship of *The Hindustan Times* that Kum Kum Chaddha who had become one of my favourites on the staff asked me, "Sir, I want you to meet my closest friend. She wants to meet you."

After 14 years of coming and going in each other's homes and despite my protesting Kum Kum continues to address me as "Sir". So does Kamna. She goes one further. She never uses my name even to third parties, "Can I speak to Sir?"

The next day Kum Kum brought Kamna over to my office and left her there for us to get to know each other. I found her uncommonly beautiful in the classical Indian mould like an Ajanta fresco.

She was a couple of inches taller than me. Long, lustrous, jet-black hair falling down to her hips. Neither very fair nor very dark but light *café-au-lait* complexion. Beautiful neck, middle-sized bosom, very slender waist with her flat belly displaying her belly button and unusually broad hips designed to accommodate a brood of children.

I gathered that she was from Patna; her father was into Urdu poetry; she could quote Urdu and Hindi poetry with equal fluency. Her mother had been a minister in the Bihar Government but due to poor health had retired from politics.

She was not very close to her parents but was devoted to her younger brother Raju. Her elder brother was married to Babu Jagjivan Ram's daughter but she rarely saw him.

She lived alone in Delhi and worked for a Gujarati firm engaged in the export of ready-made garments and semi-precious stones.

I did not get all these facts at the very first meeting but after many sessions of interrogations because Kamna was also a very private person and inexplicably secretive about small things.

I invited Kamna to come to my house with Kum Kum. I knew she had to have my wife's approval to become a regular visitor. She came and soon won over the affections of the entire family including our servants.

But it was only with me that she shared her confidences. Gradually, I became a father figure. She often sat on the floor beside my chair. I rested my hand on her silken soft shoulders as she poured out her heart to me. She never opened up completely but always held something back for the next meeting.

Kamna had a way with people, both men and women, which drew them towards her. She was also very touchy on certain matters and took offence when no offence was meant.

She was particularly sensitive that being attractive, living alone and in some style she might give men the wrong idea about her availability.

She was often in our home in the evening at drinking time. I looked forward to her fixing my Scotch. Although a strict teetotaller she knew how much was good for me. Once there were some other people present when I asked her to give me a drink and referred to her as my *saqi* (wine-server).

She was furious. She said nothing to me at the time but turned up next day to berate me in no uncertain language that I had made her out into some kind of a bimbo. I protested that I had used the word with affection as I had for Harjeet and Sadia who often saved me from pouring my own Scotch and soda.

She remained un-understanding and inconsolable. I apologised to her but felt uneasy that if she could so utterly misunderstand my affection our friendship would not last long. She forgave me and peace was restored.

Kamna became a favourite with my friends, male and female. To Prem Kirpal who has a genius for mispronouncing names she remains Ramnam. Other friends taken up by her was the GM telephones, B.M. Khanna, and his wife Rama. But not everyone took to her.

Anees Jung could not understand why I liked Kamna and tried to dismiss her as a very light-weight person. Once when we found ourselves together in Bombay in the same hotel with Kamna and Kum Kum in the adjoining room, Smita Patil, the celebrated film star, rang me up to say she wanted to see me.

As editor of *The Illustrated Weekly of India* I had put Smita on the cover page after seeing her first film and referred to her as the actress of the future. Smita wanted to come to thank me personally for having built her up.

Anees happened to drop in and was determined to meet Smita. Kamna was equally determined to see that Smita should see me alone. A lively slanging match began between the two.

After ignoring Kamna's presence, Anees abruptly turned to her and said, "Why don't you go back to your room?" Kamna snapped back, "Why should I? Why don't you leave Sir alone. Smita does not want to meet you, she wants to meet Sir." I don't recall how the tussle ended. Smita came, spent a few minutes with us and departed. A few months later she was dead.

Being, as I have said before, uncommonly attractive and instinctively generous, Kamna attracted a lot of men and women towards her. Women came and went: first there was Kum Kum, then a toughy called Chaudhry, then Sadia.

Men were more abiding. She had many suitors. She kept them at a respectable distance. But she did want to marry and beget children. She went through a half-hearted engagement with a clean-shaven Sardar living in Kuwait. It came to nothing as Kamna was determined to live in India.

Then there was a German, unhappily married and with two children. He fell desperately in love with Kamna and promised to divorce his wife to marry her.

Another engagement ceremony with Hindu rites took place in her apartment. She even spent a couple of weeks in Germany to see how she would fit in as a *hausfrau*. She returned to Delhi disillusioned and disengaged.

She was drawn towards the painter M.F. Hussain and enjoyed the attention he paid her. He made several portraits of her, and at her persistence made two of mine. They, including one of mine, decorate her home.

Then he started to take her for granted. She gave him a short shrift and refused to talk to him. Hussain pleaded with me to beg her to forgive him. She did so at her own terms. He dedicated his autobiography to her. They are friends again.

Much as I loved Kamna I wanted to see her married and bear children. She eyed a lovely, large painting in my home and asked me to give it to her. "I will give it to you as a wedding present," I told her. She took it away without getting married. She liked a large terracota Ganpati that Anoop Sarkar had given me. I again promised to give it to her as a wedding present. Once again she took it without getting married.

When she finally decided to get married, she sprung it as a surprise. She asked me over for a meal to meet a very special friend she had made. This was the tall, handsome, bearded Englishman Michael Battye of *Reuters*.

I could see with half-an-eye that he was deeply in love with Kamna and she with him. I had my doubts about their marrying as she knew nothing of his background or his career prospects. She left that part of Michael to me. I invited him over to see me. The next day I asked him what any father of a girl would like to know about his prospective son-in-law.

Michael had no private property nor much of a bank balance. He had good prospects of getting to the top in *Reuters* but that would involve many postings away from India and finally settling down in England.

I couldn't see Kamna, an elegant hostess, scrubbing floors, cooking and washing dishes in a flat in London's suburbs. A father-in-law-to-be should ask his son-in-law-to-be to produce a physical fitness certificate. That was too delicate a subject and Michael was not wanting in health and handsomeness.

I told Kamna I approved of him but was not sure if she could make a home in England. However, a marriage date was fixed. I agreed to perform *Kanyadaan*.

I had to go to Assam to preside over a literacy conference at Sibsagar. Chief Minister Hiteshwar Sakia assured he would get me back to Delhi in time for the nuptials. Indian Airlines decided otherwise. My flight from Calcutta to Delhi was delayed by six hours.

I returned home after the Kamna-Michael wedding with Hindu rites was over. Kamna's parents had come over from Patna to give her away to her English groom.

A week later a civil marriage was performed in my apartment where Michael's parents were present. Rani Jethmalani and I signed the certificate as witnesses.

Kamna moved out of her spacious apartment to a more spacious bungalow rented by *Reuters*. She went to England with Michael, spent a few weeks with his parents and sister. They bought an apartment in Belsize Park in North London.

Even so I could not reconcile myself to Kamna living anywhere else except Delhi and going out of my life forever.

I am unable to analyse my affection for Kamna. It is much more than her physical appearance. She is a giver not a taker. For whatever I gave her (or she extracted from me) she returned twice over in gifts to my wife, daughter and grand-daughter. Anything my wife wanted done, she could rely on Kamna to have it done and with difficulty pay her the cost.

Perhaps the most important factor was her faith and trust in me that evoked my affection for her. I dread the day when Michael will get orders transferring him to some other country.

Without Kamna, Delhi will not be the same.

Prema Subramaniam

Prema, my *rakhi* sister: The most loveable woman in my life.

One thing about Prema was that you could not get angry with her. She meant well and was of such a happy disposition that a harsh word would be wounding.

There were a few women in my life who I never met. Every Raksha Bandhan I received some *rakhis* from them. I wrote back to thank them and to some I sent my latest publication as a gift. Some were Punjabis, some Gujaratis, some Bengalis. One of them was a Tamilian, Prema Subramaniam, living with her engineer husband in Coimbatore.

With one *rakhi* she sent me a note saying her husband had been transferred to Bangalore and if I ever happend to be there, she would be happy to meet me. I had no idea how old she was, what she looked like, whether or not she had children, nor how her husband would react to her *rakhi* brother.

It so happened that I was due to go to Mysore a week later and would disembark at Bangalore airport to take the car sent to drive me to my destination. I wrote to Prema giving my flight number and time of arrival in Bangalore. Knowing the state of our postal services I was not sure if she would get my letter in time to meet me.

There were several Sikhs on the flight including a tall man in military uniform. Three of them were ahead of me in the line entering Bangalore airport. I noticed a short, somewhat fat woman in her 30s with a layer of snow-white in her black hair. She first approached the military man. He shrugged her off pointing backwards to the crowd following him. She approached the next Sardarji. He likewise shook her off.

I guessed she was looking for me. I went to her and said, "You must be Prema Subramaniam". She promptly dropped down to her knees to touch my feet in the South Indian fashion. I raised her by her shoulders and kissed her on both cheeks. "This is the way we greet people in the North," I said.

Our first meeting was very brief, no more than ten minutes. I promised to ring her up when I returned from Mysore to catch my return flight to Delhi.

Two days later I was back in Bangalore staying at the state guest house. I rang up Prema. She had no car and lived a long way away in the suburbs. I sent a car to fetch her. We spent a couple of hours getting to know each other's background.

She turned out to be the daughter of R.S. Mani whom I had briefly met when he was an ambassador. Her mother lived in Madras. Her brothers had migrated to the United States. She had no children and had been told by her gynaecologist she would never have any. That did not seem to depress her. She bubbled with happy laughter.

I noticed how her dark skin glowed like polished bronze and how pearl white her teeth were. She doused herself liberally with cologne and ended every sentence with a query "so what?"

A spasmodic correspondence started between us. Whenever I was in Bangalore she invited me to her home for a meal and came to take me out shopping and dined with me. She was an excellent cook and introduced me to several South Indian delicacies like *thayeer saadam* and varieties of *idlis*. She wrote out recipes and gave me home-ground *masalas* to take home for my wife.

Her husband was a mild-mannered gentleman who enjoyed his Sunday morning beer and watching TV. He was a highly qualified engineer but had not found a job with the pay he deserved.

And Prema was a spendthrift who ran out of her monthly allowance by the second week of the month. She also loved gold jewellery. When dining out with me she enjoyed non-vegetarian food. The only drink she liked was cognac.

In my visits I brought her a bottle of cologne and one or two cognacs to keep at home. In return she loaded me with gifts for me and the family: embroidered handkerchief and pillow cases, silver and walnut wood bowls. Her spending was chaotic.

Once when I was invited by Chief Minister Ramakrishna Hegde to see what I wanted of the state he ruled, I opted for wild life resorts and ancient ruins. Prema got her husband's permission to accompany me.

We drove with our escorts to Nagarhole sanctuary. At sunset we were driven through the forest and saw herds of Gaur and deer. From the top of an observation post we watched a huge tusker with its harem of she-elephants and their babies sporting by a large pond.

Back in our bungalow-cum-hostel, Prema overindulged herself with food and drink and was taken sick. I thought I would have to cancel the rest of my trip and take her back home. The next morning she was as merry as a lark full of song and laughter.

She had made friends with all the other visitors and was exchanging addresses with them. We proceeded to Hassan. She put on her tape recorder at full blast, sang with it and talked at the top of her voice. I almost went round the bend and pitied her husband who had to put up with such exuberance every day.

Fortunately at Hasan there was load-shedding and the batteries of her cassette-player had run out. No lights, no air-conditioners, no fans. The heat was sweltering. We ate a tepid meal by candle light and slept with our doors and windows wide open.

I was fagged out but Prema was as wide awake as ever. I heard her indulge in chatter and laughter with our escorts till late hours. I hoped my next-day journey would be quieter.

I had not reckoned with Prema's resourcefulness. When I was having my breakfast she went to the bazaar and got new batteries for her cassette player.

She had a stock of Mehdi Hasan's and Ghulam Ali's *ghazals* which she had specially bought for me. I simply had to listen to them. And though she did not know a word of Urdu she insisted on my explaining them to her and accompanying the maestro's singing.

I did not see much of the countryside nor the ancient ruins we visited. Prema demanded, and got, my full attention.

Prema and her husband shifted to Madras where her mother had her own little bungalow standing around coconut palms in Besant Nagar. Prema got a job as a sales assistant with Higginbothams. She made close friends with her senior colleagues. Prema was deliriously happy.

Her husband got a job in California. The few times I met her in Madras she was busy all day at the bookstore. Although she managed to sell more books than any of her colleagues, more than half of her salary was eaten up by scooter and bus fares. Nothing seemed to get her spirits down. By now they had begun to overflow on paper.

Her letter would often run into 30 pages with writings on the margins. Very little of her outpouring apart from my name on the envelope were addressed to me or gave any news of what she was doing. There were reams of poetry and lyrical prose most of it taken from books. She did not wait for replies. To my weekly letter of a few paragraphs she could send four to five a week.

Every time I went to Madras Prema was at the airport with a thermos flask of chilled coconut water which she knew I liked and accompanied me to my host Sunny Malhan's house. She spent the day with me, made me buy bulbs and seeds for her garden and a sari after I had bought one for my daughter.

She was as lavish with my purse as she was with her husband's who sent her a handsome cheque every month. She saw to it that by the end of the month there was nothing left in her account.

Once again I made the mistake of letting her bring her cassette player and picnic basket when we went to visit the snake and crocodile farm on the way to Mahabalipuram. It was music at full blast all the way.

On the way back she insisted on having a picnic lunch in a shady groove. Within a few minutes we were surrounded by village urchins. No amount of shouting *Poh, Poh* drove them away. We gave them most of what Prema had brought and returned to Madras.

One thing about Prema was that you could not get angry with her. She meant well and was of such a happy disposition that a harsh word would be wounding.

Prema's religion was as mixed up as she. She went to temples, churches and *dargahs*. In her own home she had a *pooja* room where deities of different faiths were represented on the altar: many of the gods and goddesses of the Hindu pantheon, Jain Mahavira, the Buddha, Jesus Christ and after getting to know me, Guru Nanak.

She visited the Sikh temple in Madras and had a marble tablet put in the wall invoking the Guru's blessings on me. Her favourite God was Murugan.

Once, when she stayed in Delhi with us on her way to the United States, she prostrated herself on the carpet at my wife's feet. She was not interested in visiting monuments and instead spent the afternoon at Hanuman Mandir.

Having successfully dodged a few attempts to get her to the United States, Prema was faced with the possibility of losing her Green Card. She could no longer resist the pressure put on her by her husband and family all of whom had made their home in America.

Last year Prema resigned her job with Higginbothams and left for New York. There is little chance of my seeing her for the next five years. Her letters have become shorter as she has to write on air-letter forms. She still keeps sending us gifts. But I expect with the passage of years they too will get scarcer.

In another four years Prema will have become an American citizen. I can't think of another person 200 per cent authentic Tamilian Brahmin make peace with the American way of life. She was the most unlikely woman to come into my life. And the most loveable.

10 Amrita Shergil

Amrita vowed to seduce me but that day never came.

She was said to have given appointments to her lovers with two-hour intervals — at times six to seven a day — before she retired for the night. If this was true (men's gossip is less reliable than women's) love formed very little part of Amrita's life. Sex was what mattered to her. She was a genuine case of nymphomania...

I am hardly justified in describing Amrita Shergil as a woman in my life. I met her only twice. But these two meetings remain imprinted in my memory. Her fame as an artist, her glamour as a woman of great beauty which she gave credence to in some of her self-portraits, and her reputation for promiscuity snowballed into a veritable avalanche which hasn't ended to this day and gives me an excuse to include her in my list.

One summer, her last, I heard that she and her Hungarian cousin-husband who was a doctor had taken an apartment across the road where I lived in Lahore. He meant to set up a medical practice, she, her painting studio. Why they chose to make their home in Lahore, I have no idea. She had a large number of friends and admirers in the city. She also had rich, landowning relatives on her Sikh father's side who regularly visited Lahore. It was as good a place for them to start their lives and any in India.

It was the month of June 1941. My wife had taken our seven-month-old son, Rahul, for the summer to my parents' house "Sunderban" in Mashobra, seven miles beyond Simla. I spent my mornings in the High Court gossiping with lawyers over cups of coffee or listening to cases being argued before judges. I had hardly any case to handle myself. Nevertheless, I made it a point to wear my black coat, white tabs round the collar and carry my black gown with me to give others an appearance of being very busy. I returned home for lunch and a long siesta before I went to play tennis at the Cosmopolitan Club.

One afternoon I came home to find my flat full of aroma of expensive French perfume. In my sitting room-cum-library on the table was a silver tankard of chilled beer. I tiptoed to the kitchen, asked my cook about the visitor. "A memsahib in a sari," he informed me. He had told her I would be back any moment for lunch. She had helped herself to a bottle of beer from the fridge and was in the bathroom to freshen up. I had little doubt my uninvited visitor could be no other than Amrita Shergil.

For several weeks before her arrival in Lahore I had heard stories of her exploits during her previous visits to the city before she had married her cousin. She usually stayed in Faletti's Hotel. She was said to have given appointments to her lovers with two-hour intervals — at times six to seven a day — before she retired for the night. If this was true (men's gossip is less reliable than women's) love formed very little part of Amrita's life. Sex was what mattered to her. She was a genuine case of nymphomania, and according to her nephew Vivian Sunderam's published account, she was also a lesbian. Her *modus vivendi* is vividly described by Badruddin Tyabji in his memoirs. One winter when he was staying in Simla he invited Amrita for dinner. He had a fire lit for protection from cold and European classical music playing on his gramophone. He wasted the first evening talking of literature and music. He invited her again. He had the same log fire and the same European classical music. Before he knew what was happening, Amrita simply took her clothes off and lay stark naked on the carpet. She did not believe in wasting time. Even the very proper Badruddin Tyabji got the message.

Years later Malcolm Muggeridge, the celebrated author, told me that he had spent a week in Amrita's parents' home in Summer Hill, Simla. He was then in the prime of his youth — early 20s. In a week she had reduced him to a limp rag. "I could not cope with her," he admitted. "I was glad to get back to Calcutta."

A woman with the kind of reputation Amrita enjoyed drew men towards her like iron filings to a magnet. I was no exception. As she entered the room, I stood up to greet her. "You must be Amrita Shergil," I said. She nodded. Without apologising for helping herself to my beer she proceeded to tell me why she had come to see me. They were mundane matters which robbed our first meeting of all romance. She wanted to know about plumbers, *dhobis*, carpenters, cooks, bearers, etc., she could hire in the neighbourhood. While she talked I had a good look at her. Short, sallow complexioned, black hair severely parted in the middle; thick sensual lips covered with bright red lipstick; stubby nose with black-heads visible. Passably good looking but by no means a beauty.

Her self-portraits were exercises in narcissism. She probably had as nice a figure as she portrayed herself in her nudes but I had no means of knowing what she concealed beneath her sari. What I can't forget is her brashness. After she had finished talking she looked around the room. I pointed to a few paintings and said, "These are by my wife; she is an amateur." She glanced at them and scoffed, "That is obvious." I was taken aback by her disdain but did not know how to retort. More was to come.

A few weeks later I joined my family in Mashobra. Amrita was staying with the Chaman Lals who had rented a house above my father's. I invited them for lunch. The three of them, Chaman, his wife Helen and Amrita came at mid-day. The lunch table and chairs were lined on a platform under the shade of a holly-oak tree which overlooked the hillside and a vast valley. My seven-month-old son was in the play-pen teaching himself how to stand up on his feet. He was a lovely child with curly brown locks and large questioning eyes. Everyone took turns to talk to him and compliment my wife for producing such a beautiful boy. Amrita remained lost in the depths of her beer mug. When everyone had finished she gave the child a long look and remarked, "What an ugly little boy!" Everyone froze. Some protested at the unkind remark. But Amrita was back drinking her beer. After our guests had departed my wife said to me very firmly, "I am not having that bloody bitch in my house again."

Amrita's bad behaviour became the talk of Simla's social circle. So did my wife's comment on her. Amrita got to know what my wife had said and told people, "I will teach that bloody woman a lesson she won't forget; I will seduce her husband."

I eagerly awaited the day of seduction. It never came. We were back in Lahore in the autumn. So were Amrita and her husband across the road. One night her cousin Gurcharan Singh (Channi) who owned a large orange orchard near Gujranwala turned up and asked if he could spend the night with us as Amrita who had asked him for the weekend was too ill to have him stay with her. The next day other friends of Amrita's dropped in. They told us that Amrita was in a coma and her parents were coming down from Summer Hill to be with her. She was an avid bridge player and in her semi-conscious moments mumbled bridge calls. The next morning I heard Amrita was dead.

I hurried to her apartment. Her father, Sardar Umrao Singh Shergil, stood by the door in a state of daze mumbling a prayer. Her Hungarian mother went in and out of the room where her daughter lay dead unable to comprehend what had happened. That afternoon no more than a dozen men and women followed Amrita's corètge to the cremation ground. Her husband lit her funeral pyre. When we returned to her apartment the police was waiting for her husband. Britain had declared war on Hungary as ally of its enemy, Nazi Germany. Amrita's husband had become an enemy national and had to be detained in prison.

He was lucky to be in police custody. A few days later his mother-in-law, Amrita's mother, started a campaign against him accusing him of murdering her daughter. She sent letters to everyone she knew asking for a full investigation into the circumstances of her daughter's sudden death. I was one of them. Murder it certainly was not; negligence perhaps. I got details from Dr. Raghubir Singh who was our family doctor and the last person to see Amrita alive. He told me that he had been summoned at midnight. Amrita had peritonitis caused perhaps by a clumsy abortion. She had bled profusely. Her husband asked Dr. Raghubir Singh to give her blood transfusion. The doctor refused to do so without fully examining his patient. While the two doctors were arguing with each other, Amrita quietly slipped out of life. As they say, her fame liveth even more.

11

Reeta Devi Varma

Quite unabashed I describe her as my current heartthrob.

She was draped in a plain white sari. She had high cheek bones the same as some eastern people have. No make-up, no jewellery. Fair skinned, tall, slender and beautifully proportioned with a long neck, full bosom, slender waist and long legs. She looked more like a professional model than a housewife living in a middle class locality...

Members of my family describe her as "Papa's latest". Quite unabashed I describe her as my current heartthrob. There is a mere 40 years age difference between us. She is happily married to a handsome aristocrat, one of the Cooch-Behar family and a nephew of Rajmata Gayatri Devi of Jaipur. Such trivia do not matter much to me. Looks do. Personality does. And this young lady has both in plenty.

I first noticed her standing at the gate of Sujan Singh Park in a small crowd that had collected to see L. K. Advani's motorised chariot go by on its journey from Somnath to

Ayodhya. Much as I had admired Advani I strongly disapproved of this exercise. I was out there only out of curiosity to see what response the people of Delhi were giving him. It was a ragtag procession of no more than a couple of hundred shouting slogans. Someone on Advani's chariot recognised me standing among the bystanders and promptly announced my name over the loudspeaker as one of their well-wishers.

Advani waved to me! I waved back to him and turned away in disgust to return to my apartment. From my window I saw a lady draped in a plain white sari go by. I noticed she had high cheek bones the same as some eastern people have. No make-up, no jewellery. Fair skinned, tall, slender and beautifully proportioned with a long neck, full bosom, slender waist and long legs. She looked more like a professional model than a housewife living in a middle-class locality like Sujan Singh Park. The next morning I met her on the road again. She spoke to me first. "Sir, can I take the liberty of dropping in and getting you to autograph some of your books for me?"

"Welcome anytime you like! Nothing flatters an author more than autographing his books", I replied and asked, "Where do you live?"

"Sir, I am in the next block to yours. We are neighbours," she said. "I know your daughter, son-in-law; your nephew Tejbir and his wife Mala. I didn't have the courage to introduce myself". I saw her glide along and disappear into the neighbouring block.

Who was she? How was it that I had not noticed her before?

I made enquiries from the staff of Sujan Singh Park. They knew her as *Kuttey Waalee Memsahib* — the lady with the dogs. It transpired that she had six or seven stray dogs she had picked up from the roads to give them a home. I fall for dog-lovers, more for those who don't bother about pedigrees but have genuine affection for all animals including the lame and the one-eyed. I was told that her husband was also a dog-lover and went out every evening in his car carrying packets of meat and *roti* cooked by his wife to give to stray dogs in the locality. The staff people did not know their names — only *Kuttey Waalee*.

A few days later she came to get some books signed. She asked me to put her name down in the books and autograph them. Her name was Reeta. "Reeta what?" I asked her. "Just Reeta. That's enough," she replied, "but if you want to know, I am Reeta Devi Varma. My husband, Bheem, is in business." She was not very forthcoming. I wanted to know more about her family, where she had been educated, what she was doing before she became *Kuttey Waalee* and what else she did beside caring for dogs. Above all, why someone as good looking as she had not gone into films or modelling. I discovered a second loveable aspect of her character. Unlike most good-lookers who look for excuses to fish for compliments, Reeta avoided talking about herself. It was from others that I found out that she had been a model and had for a time been Air India's most sought after air-hostess. Whenever Mrs. Gandhi went abroad, Reeta was assigned to look after her. Amongst her admirers was the chief connoisseur of air-hostesses, the young and handsome tycoon of Bombay Dyeing, Nusli Wadia.

It was Bhupen Hazarika, the noted Assamese singer, who filled me with details of Reeta's childhood. She was the daughter of one Mrs. Roy, a botanist who was for twelve years principal of Cotton College, Guwahati. Hazarika told me that students took botany as their subject just to be able to ogle at Mrs. Roy who was a stunning beauty. Reeta was Bengali-Assamese, a Goswami on her mother's side from which she inherited her looks. Her parents had separated a long time ago. For many years Reeta was the toast of Calcutta's social circles.

Reeta could have married any man she wanted. She chose Bheem Varma, a scion of the princely family of Cooch-Behar then in tea business. She picked up the mannerisms of members of aristocratic Rajput families. Whenever I asked her over to have a drink in the evening, she refused to take Scotch because she knew it was difficult to come by and expensive and preferred to fix a glass of Indian rum for herself. She quite liked serving me drinks. She would give the glass to me with both her hands as if presenting a *nazrana* to her overlord. It took me quite some time and bullying to make her give me the tumbler with one hand. And to this day, after four years of knowing her, she still addresses me as 'Sir' and has never uttered my name.

Reeta is by no means short of conversation. She can chat on endlessly but the range of her topics is very restricted. She has been for years associated with Mother Teresa and is a regular visitor to the institutions run by the Missionaries of Charity. She can be very critical of society ladies who squander their wealth and energy at both the kitty and cocktail parties. At the same time she loves entertaining, is a great cook and her parties go on till the early hours of the morning. It does not occur to her that that is also a waste of time and energy.

In recent years she got interested in politics and became a kind of resident spokesperson for Assam and its Chief Minister Hiteswar Saikia. Because of her I have become half-Assamese and visit Assam every other month. She got me invited in Mother Teresa's project to set up the first AIDS and TB rehabilitation centre in Guwahati. She pressurised Saikia to grant 14 acres of land near Guwahati airport, had him give Mother Teresa title deeds to the land and an initial grant of Rs.5 lakhs to get the project going. She nagged me into writing letters to industrialists to make donations.

From Reeta's own mouth I heard of her explosive temper. She is tall and strong ever ready to hammer any man who she thinks deserves being hammered. Once her Sardarji neighbour with an American wife was upset by the incessant barking of her dogs. In his irritation he hit one of them with his walking stick. Reeta flew at him, gave him a tongue-lashing and reported him to the police. The poor Sardarji fled to his apartment with his tail between his legs. I dread the day when she loses her temper with me. I have no forgiveness for ill-tempered people and quickly opt out of any further association with them. So far she has only once expressed displeasure over my accepting an invitation of someone she particularly disliked. She nagged me about it for over an hour. Like most women, Reeta is possessive about her friends. I let her nag me till she ran out of arguments.

I like being seen out with Reeta. It does something to my morale. At times she has been taken to be my grand-daughter. That does not bother me because I have a pretty grand-daughter. However, friends have begun to gossip about my latest infatuation. "It won't last very long", said a lady who has known Reeta for much longer than I have. "Most men get taken up by Reeta when they meet her first. After a while they drop her because she has very little to say. Or says the same things over and over again."

I have no intention of dropping Reeta because I find myself on the same side as her. I love animals, she cares for them. I disapprove of communal politicians, she hates them to the extent of picking quarrels with them and abusing people who write against Muslims or Christians. I admire people who work among the poor. She does.

Once she took me to a home for destitute, handicapped children run by the Missionaries of Charity in Jangpura. While I was patting the head of a little blind girl who was clinging to my legs, Reeta picked up a one-year-old spastic child. The boy got very excited and urinated on Reeta's hand and soiled her sari. Reeta did not flinch. She held the child till he had finished urinating. Then she handed him over to an attendant to be cleansed and put back in bed. That one incident put Reeta Devi Varma in a class apart from any other woman in my life.

12

The Beggar Maid

A vision arising from the rain water.

Fair, beautifully proportioned, uncombed hair wildly scattered about her face, a dirty white dhoti *untidly draped around her body: I gazed at her for quite some time and wondered what an attractive young woman was doing in this vice-ridden city. I fantasised about her long into the night.*

For the first few months after taking over the editorship of *The Illustrated Weekly of India* I lived as a paying guest of a young Parsi couple in a flat in Churchgate. I did not know many people, so had very little social life. I walked to office every morning and walked back every evening as I refused to use the car and chauffeur provided for me.

Among the earliest friends I made was A.G. Noorani who combined practising law with journalism. He was and is a bachelor. We began to spend our evenings together: we would go for a stroll along Marine Drive and return to my flat.

I had my evening ration of Scotch; Noorani who was and is a teetotaller had a glass of aerated water. Then we set out to try different restaurants in the neighbourhood. After dinner we tried different *paanwallahs* and bade each other good night. This routine was upset with the onset of the monsoon in Bombay when I ran into the lady about whom I write today.

There was a break in the downpour. I was alone as I stepped out of a restaurant. A gas station and a few shops were on my way home. I stopped there to buy myself a *paan* and chatted with a *bhelpuriwallah* and asked him how was his business during the rains: not very well, he admitted. "*Magar iski kismat jaag jatee hai*" (her fortune increases) he added pointing to a woman sitting on the steps of a shop nearby. "What I can't sell, I give to her. She is a beggar. *Thori paagal hai* (she is a little mad)." I looked at the woman hungrily gulping *bhelpuri*. An uncommonly attractive girl, she was in her mid-twenties.

Fair, beautifully proportioned, uncombed hair wildly scattered about her face, a dirty white *dhoti* untidily draped around her body: I gazed at her for quite some time and wondered what an attractive young woman was doing alone in this vice-ridden city. I fantasised about her long into the night.

Thereafter I made it a point to buy my after-dinner *paan* from the same *paanwallah* by the gas station, exchanged a few words with the *bhelpuriwallah* as I ogled at the beggar maid on the steps of the closed shop. I often saw her talking to herself. I tried to buy *bhelpuri* to give to the girl, but the stall-owner rejected my offer. He had plenty of left-overs and feeding the girl was his monopoly.

One evening while I was at dinner the clouds burst in all their fury and roads around Churchgate were flooded. I tucked my trousers up to my knees, took my sandals in my hands, unfurled my umbrella to save my turban and waded through the swirling muddy water. Both the *paanwallah* and the *bhelpuriwallah* had shut shop and gone home. I saw the beggar girl stretched out on the marble steps barely an inch above the stream of rain water running past her. She couldn't have had anything to eat that night. I was sorely tempted to give her some money but was not sure how she would react. I walked home thinking about her, and thought about her into the late hours of the night.

It poured all through the night. As I woke up to look out of the window which overlooked the maidan with the Rajabhai clock tower on the other side, the rain was still coming down in sheets. The maidan was flooded. I saw the shadowy figure of a woman walking across the maidan with a tin in hand. I saw her hike her wet dhoti and start splashing water between her buttocks. I trained my field glasses on her. She turned to look if any one was around. Having reassured herself that she wasn't being watched she took off her dhoti and stood stark naked in the pouring rain. It was my beggar woman. She poured dirty water on her body, rubbed her bosom, waist, arms and legs. The "bath" over she put the wet dhoti back on her and sloshed her way back towards Churchgate station.

The vision of Venus arising out of the sea in the form of a beggar maid of Bombay haunted me for many days that I was away in Delhi. When I returned to Bombay I made it a point to go to Churchgate for my after-dinner stroll. The *paanwallah* and the *bhelpuriwallah* were there. But not the beggar. I asked the *bhelpuriwallah* what had happened to girl. His eyes filled with tears and his voice choked as he replied: "*Saaley bharooay utha ke lay gaye*" (the bloody pimps abducted her).

Part Two

MEN

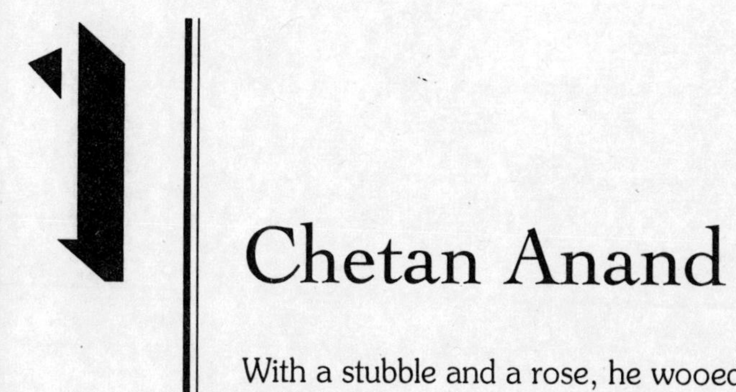

Chetan Anand

With a stubble and a rose, he wooed all the pretty women.

People can be divided into givers and takers, suckers and spongers. Chetan Anand was the biggest taker and sponger I met in my life.

In the two years I was in Government College, Lahore, I got to know a lot of people who later made it to the top, or near the top, in the film industry.

Two years senior to me was Balraj Sahni. His younger brother Bhisham, B.R. Chopra and Chetan Anand were in the same class with me. A few years junior were Dev Anand and Uma Kashyap who as Kamini Kaushal rose to the top. Another junior contemporary was I.S. Johar who was in Forman Christian College. Most of these men and women re-emerged in my life in later years. But the closest to me in Lahore days was Chetan Anand. He was quite a character.

Chetan Anand was a pretty boy with curly hair and soulful eyes. He was much sought after by tough lads who fancied effeminate males.

Chetan avoided them like the plague and attached himself to me. Although tongues wagged, there was nothing homosexual about our relationship. We walked from our hostel to college together, sat side by side in our classes, played tennis and went to the pictures.

Like me he too aspired to get into the ICS and came to England to sit for the exams. Neither of us made the grade.

I returned to Lahore with a law degree. He had no more than the BA he had taken from the Punjab University. He was desperately looking for a job.

He spent a summer in my apartment. I saw another side to Chetan. Women found him very attractive and he had a unique approach of ingratiating himself in their favour. On the hottest days in June he would go out wearing his overcoat, a stubble on his chin and with a single flower in his hand call on his lady friends. Inevitably the dialogue opened with the young lady asking him why he was wearing an overcoat. "This is all I possess in the world," he would reply as he presented her with the single flower in his hand. He had phenomenal success.

In due course he succeeded in winning the heart of the most sought after girl in the university, Uma Chatterjee. Though she was Christian she defied her parents and agreed to marry a Hindu boy who till then had no job.

I threw a large party to celebrate their engagement. I discovered fickleness in Chetan's character. He flirted outrageously with other girls in the party. Next morning when I reprimanded him and called him a *harami* he smiled disarmingly and brushed away my protests. They were married, had two children. Uma could not take his philandering any longer and left him for Alkazi. Chetan shacked up with a Sikh girl young enough to be his daughter.

We continued to see each other. I wrote to him about his films. He only made one good one.

He produced the *son et lumière* programmes on the Delhi Red Fort based on the script written by me. I heard that he claimed to have written the text as well but when I questioned him he denied ever having made the claim. (Later there were others who made similar claims.)

When I moved to Bombay to take up the editorship of *The Illustrated Weekly of India*, I looked forward to renewing acquaintance with friends of my Lahore days who had become big names in the film world. Most of all with Chetan Anand who had enjoyed my hospitality on innumerable occasions and been closest to me.

I spent many weekends in Balraj Sahni's villa in Juhu. B.R. Chopra asked me to his home a couple of times as did Kamini Kaushal. Once a week I dined with I.S. Johar and his ex-wife Rama Bans. Even Dev Anand invited me to his large cocktail parties. But Chetan Anand whom I expected to see more than anyone else remained mysteriously silent.

He rang me up a few times when he wanted publicity for something he was doing and usually ended the dialogue with the vague: '*Kabhi hamare ghar aana*' (drop in some day).

I was disappointed and angry. A few months before I was due to leave Bombay, I ran into Chetan and his lady friend at a party. She asked me: "Why haven't you come to our home?" I exploded: "Because I have never been asked by that *kameena* friend of yours." Chetan turned to make light of it. "Sardar you are very angry with me. When will you come?"

I couldn't take it any more. "Never," I yelled back. "You are a *besharam matlabee* (shameless self-seeker). It never occurred to you to return the months of my hospitality you enjoyed."

People can be divided into givers and takers, suckers and spongers. Chetan Anand was the biggest taker and sponger I met in my life.

2 Romesh Chander

The Charlie boy no one knew after
a lifetime of intimacy.

During his courtship days we saw quite a lot of him and were regularly briefed on how his courtship was proceeding. It was a roller-coaster ride. One day he would be riding on cloud nine, the next day in the dumps and would break down in tears.

I wrote a short story based on Romesh Chander, or Charles as we used to call him in Government College, Lahore. It is in my first compilation of short stories *The Mark of Vishnu* under the title "The Butterfly" because of the many changes in his personality from the chrysalis to a full-fledged butterfly. He was furious and threatened to take me to court. He had second thoughts about it as I made him out as a hero of sorts, which he was not.

Charles came to Government College from Bishop Cotton School, Simla, which was largely an Anglo-Indian institution. He was a natty little fellow and as much of a Brown Sahib as he could be in his five-foot-four-inch height. He wore a pith solar topee sporting a pheasant feather on one side and a strap to go under his chin. He wore it at an angle as Anglo boys did. His speech, like theirs, was punctuated with "yes mun, no mun." He did not much care to mingle with us natives and preferred to be with the handful of Anglo-Indian boys who made it to the Government College. He tried to enter their social circle in Lahore, which was centred around the railway colony.

He soon discovered that having nothing Anglo about him except his speech, he was not welcome. He had no option but to seek the friendship of natives who could speak his lingo. I was one of them. At first he liked to be known as Charles or Charlie. After being rebuffed by the Anglo-Indian circle, he tried to drop his English name. Whenever introduced as Charles or Charlie, he would clarify "the name is Romesh Chander". He did not fully succeed in changing his identity and came to be known as Romesh Chander Charlie. We also discovered that he spoke Punjabi and Hindustani as well as any of us. His solar topee disappeared. He began to dress in *kurta-pajama*. That was his second reincarnation.

A third one was soon to emerge. A girl cousin arrived on the scene. Damyanti Batra was a most attractive young girl draped in a plain white *khadi* sari and passionately Gandhian in outlook. Every young man who met her fell in love with her. Charles was no exception. He also took to wearing *khadi* and spouting the language of freedom. He threw himself into the workers' movement and became the spokesperson of the exploited and harassed tonga drivers. He acquired yet another name — "Tongawallah Charlie" or "Charlie Tongawallah." He spent a few days in the police lock-up. The partition of India wrought yet another change in Charlie's make-up. Some members of his family stayed on in Pakistan to look after their ancestral property. They converted to Islam and became loyal Pakistanis. Charlie migrated to India, shed his leftist cocoon and became a respectable civil servant. He joined All India Radio and was also selected for the foreign service. Then for some mysterious reason perhaps connected with his past record, his name was deleted from those selected to serve abroad and he remained with AIR.

Charlie had a way with children. He loved them; they loved him. He put his children's programme of AIR on the national map. He was also very emotional. He decided to do the running commentary on Pandit Nehru's funeral. You could not hear much of what was going on because Charlie's voice was choked with sobs. It was a total disaster.

I did not know much of Charlie's love life. I knew he admired his cousin Damyanti Batra. She went on to marry M.L. Chawla, a senior executive in the I & B Ministry. It was quite some time later that he met Padma and fell head over heels in love with her. At the time Padma was not interested in Charlie and did her best to put him off. But Charlie proved to be a very persistent suitor. During his courtship days we saw quite a lot of him and were regularly briefed on how his courtship was proceeding. It was roller-coaster ride. One day he would be riding on cloud nine, the next day in the dumps and would break down in tears.

He wore out Padma's resistance and she agreed to become his wife. Charlie could not believe his good luck. Whenever he brought Padma over he was full of praise for her beauty and her talents.

Once he asked her to sing for us. She sang while Charlie watched in open-mouthed wonder as if he were listening to Lata Mangeshkar and Asha Bhosle put together. Later when alone with me, he asked me what I thought of Padma's singing. *Bilkul besura gaatee hai* (she sings totally out of tune), I told him. He was amazed at my lack of judgement. And promptly told Padma of what I had said.

Charlie could never keep anything to himself. You said everything to him in confidence; it was known to everyone the next day.

He was also a bit of a gossip and enjoyed running down people behind their backs. Soon no one in his circle of friends trusted him. But you had to give it to Charlie, he never allowed his friends to drop him. He used them when he needed them.

I don't get to see Charlie for months. But I know he is always there — living a happy domesticated life with his wife and children in Sarva Priya Vihar in south Delhi. Even after retirement he keeps himself busy as ever making programmes for broadcasting or for television. Whenever he wants Scotch or has some *matlab*, he invites himself to our house. He knows every member of my family and servants, and takes good care to talk to them. He is very affable and popular. There are no tensions when he is there. But no sooner does he leave than I start feeling uneasy about him. I have known him for over fifty years and still feel I do not really know him.

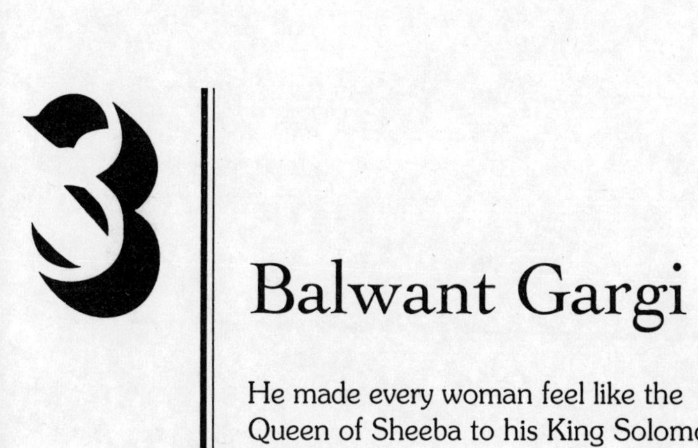

Balwant Gargi

He made every woman feel like the
Queen of Sheeba to his King Solomon.

He is short, ungainly, badly dressed, shakes his bottom when he walks; his gestures are effeminate, and is forever rubbing hands with invisible soap!

I cannot recall when and where I first met Balwant Gargi. It was sometime during my Lahore days between 1940 and 1947. I was trying to catch up on my Punjabi which I had learnt to read in my village, Hadali, and kept up to be able to read and write to my mother who knew no other language. Of its literature I knew next to nothing except a few scriptural texts which we were forced to memorise to say our prayers. I did not understand what they meant. On my return to India I tried to read Bhai Veer Singh's poetry.

While I found some of his short poems quite enchanting, I could not bring myself to share the enthusiasm Punjabi littérateurs had for his long epic poems in blank verse. His novels like those of the celebrated Nanak Singh (and believe it or not the Akali leader Master Tara Singh) I found uniformly second rate. Surely there was more to Punjabi literature than these works?

Having almost no legal work on hand, I spent more time reading classical poets and novelists of English, Urdu and Punjabi than I did my law books. As far as Punjabi was concerned, I started with the poet Mohan Singh, then professor in the newly opened Sikh National College. I found his poems way above those I had read.

I invited him home. He became a regular visitor. He introduced me to Professor Teja Singh who wrote books in Gurumukhi and English and to Kartar Singh Duggal. I expect Gargi was introduced by one of these men as an up and coming playwright and prose-writer. There were not many Hindus who wrote in the Gurumukhi script in those days. He came from a Bania family of Bhatinda and knew the Jat and the lower middle-class urban community very well. He handled the Punjabi language better than most writers of prose and spiced his narrative with wit, sarcasm and acid humour. Or maybe, I met him in the leftist circle of Lahore. He was closer to the Communist Party than I. He was perhaps a card-holder; I was a fellow traveller. I parted company with the communists much earlier than Gargi and turned into an angry critic. Gargi took his time to reject communism. We had quite a few things in common.

It was after the partition of India when we found ourselves in Delhi that we got to know each other better. His entry in my family came through my mother who only read Gurumukhi. He gave her his play *Loha Kut* (The Ironsmith) and took her to see it performed on the stage. She was charmed. Few of her husband's or children's friends took notice of her. Gargi became her friend and was welcomed at her coffee sessions. He always was an excellent raconteur and could hold everyone's interest. That was perhaps the secret of his success with women, many of whom were young and beautiful. "What is it they find in Gargi?" people asked. "He is short, ungainly, badly dressed, shakes his bottom when he walks; his gestures are effeminate, and is forever rubbing hands with invisible soap!" The answer was that he was a sympathetic listener and when it came to women, he could lay on flattery with a shovel. Each one was made to feel like the Queen of Sheeba to his King Solomon.

At the time I got to know him better, he was said to be more than friendly with the wife of a Sikh friend. Gargi had a marked preference for Sikh women. In his tiny one-room and courtyard tucked away in a narrow lane behind Scindia House (Connaught Place) I met scores of pretty girls working on the stage and in the films. One was Parveen Babi whom he brought to my home for dinner. Also writers like Amrita Pritam, Ajeet Cour and Uma Vasudev.

Gargi was often abroad, teaching drama at Seattle University, producing plays in Glasgow. I too was often abroad and away in Bombay for nine years.

In Seattle, Gargi acquired an American wife Jeannie. She was a few inches taller than him and a stunning beauty. I was totally captivated by her and often asked them over for meals. Jeannie was naïve beyond belief. She also had an enormous appetite for food. She could polish off dinner for three people without batting an eyelid. Gargi was embarrassed by her gargantuan appetite and grumbled, "People think she has nothing to eat at home." He was more disappointed that Jeannie did not bother to pick up Punjabi to be able to understand the acclaim he was getting as a dramatist.

Jeannie gave him a son and a daughter. Then the couple began to drift apart. They were living in Chandigarh where he had been appointed professor of dramatic art at the university. He fell for one of his students, a young and attractive divorcee — needless to say, a Sikh. He describes her seduction vividly in his autobiographical novel — *The Naked Triangle*. On a winter night he decided to drop the girl home in his car. In the garage lust overtook both of them. They got down to business on the garage floor. Through the window they could see Jeannie playing the piano to her children. Jeannie never forgave him for this act of betrayal and asked him for a divorce.

Gargi brought his latest girl friend to meet me in my office in Bombay. She seemed to be very enamoured of him. He was still uncertain whether or not he had done the right thing. I protested my loyalty to Jeannie.

It did not take very long for the new infatuation to cool. The lady found other admirers. The publication of *The Naked Triangle* proved to be the last straw that broke their relationship. It was easy to identify her: she was mother of two children and was made out to be a scarlet woman which she was not. I reviewed his novel and wrote that it amounted to betrayal of trust of someone he had been close to. Gossip has it that the lady turned up in Delhi, stormed into Gargi's courtyard and gave him a tongue-lashing. And more.

Gargi survived the ordeal. He even organised a meeting of the *cognoscenti* at the India International Centre to discuss his novel. He asked me to preside over it. I could never say no to Gargi. He knew he would come in for a panning, almost certainly from women in the audience. He had his one-man cohort led by the sculptor-painter-architect Satish Gujral. On his summing up Gargi displayed some of his self-esteem. "I don't care what people say about my having written so openly about a woman whose intimacy I enjoyed. But who will know about these people 50 or 100 years from now. Future generations will gauge me and the literacy merit of my work."

I take the credit for persauding Gargi to write in English. "You are like a frog croaking in a well," I told him. "How many people read your books in Gurumukhi? 500? 1000? No more. You write in English. Indians all over the country will read you. You will get an open window to the world."

He agreed. His book on Indian theatre was published in the States. Then *The Purple Moonlight* which is his memoirs based on his little home and courtyard. It shows how Gargi has mellowed over the years. His earlier profiles of his friends often had the scorpion's sting in their tails which hurt the victims for the years to come. Now he finds it hard to say anything unkind about anybody. He wants to be loved and admired.

Gargi's fortunes were always on a roller-coaster ride. Whenever he came back from abroad he had dollars to spare. He would buy a car — one time a second-hand jalopy without a roof. He would entertain his friends, buy a new camera (he is an uncommonly good photographer) and indulge himself.

The money would soon run out; the car had to be sold. His telephone would often be cut off for non-payment of bills. There were times he did not have a naya paisa in his bank account or in his pocket. His friends came to his aid.

Ethnic compulsions made him clear all his debts. Being a Bania balancing budgets was in his blood. Then he would make some serial for TV and get a whopping advance. He would buy a new car, get a new stereo-system, a new camera — and entertain his friends with Scotch and a sumptuous meal. A new lady friend would appear on the scene — usually a Sardarni.

Gargi is not the easiest person to get along with. Other creative artists often quarrel with him. He made a documentary on Yamini Krishnamurthy — who is another prickly personality. After much expense of time and money, Yamini was very critical of Gargi's work. He was heart-broken. However, after their quarrel was over, it was Yamini who invited me over to her house to see the film.

There are times when I don't hear from Gargi for months on end. When he rings up and invites himself for coffee, he usually has a purpose to fulfil: get me to review his latest book or film, build up some budding actor or actress. I know he is a bit of a *matlabee* but there is hardly anyone else whose visit I look forward to more than that of Balwant Gargi. He wastes half the mug of coffee I serve him, but he leaves me in a state of exhaltation.

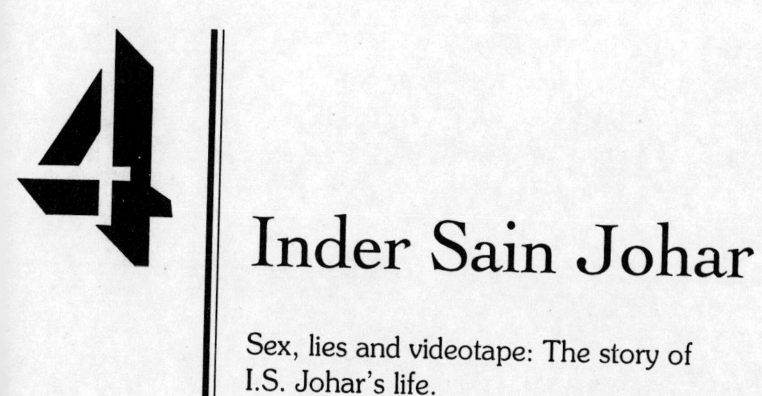

4 Inder Sain Johar

Sex, lies and videotape: The story of I.S. Johar's life.

Even more bizarre was his story of how he bedded two sisters and their mother. One sister had been his mistress for some years before she left him to get married. She introduced her younger sister to Johar and asked him to help her get into films. One evening...Johar asked her if she would like a hot cup of tea.... She replied, "if you really want to know what I would like best, I'd like a nice fuck." The girl left Johar to become a star. Her mother...one night came to his bed, stark naked. "I did not want to hurt the old lady's feelings," wrote Johar.

Inder Sain Johar was a couple of years younger than me. He was in Forman Christian College, Lahore, and was making some noise on the amateur stage as a comic actor. We had met, shaken hands, but did not get to know each other. One summer evening when I was a practising lawyer living in a small flat opposite the High Court, I heard a band playing raucous music coming down the road. I went up to my balcony to see what was happening. It was a wedding procession. On a white horse sat I.S. Johar decked up as bridegroom. He was on his way to marry Rama Bans, a very pretty girl who also acted in college plays. The couple migrated to Bombay to try their fortune in the film industry. I lost track of them. They had two children, a son and a daughter.

I saw some films in which Johar had acted, including a couple of Hollywood productions in English. I did not rate him as a great actor. When he turned from acting to directing films in which he cast himself in the main role, I formed an even poorer opinion of his histrionic talents. When he ran out of ideas, he descended to shocking people. In one film (I think it was called *Five Rifles*), he had his own daughter appear bare-breasted on the screen. I don't recall how he got round the censors. His wife Rama was disillusioned and divorced him to marry a cousin named Harbans — hence the name Rama Bans — and opened a health-cum-beauty parlour in Delhi. She was even more disillusioned with her second husband, sold her business and returned to Bombay. Her son had by then become a dope addict. Her daughter made a disastrous marriage with an Englishman who abducted their only child and smuggled him away to England. Johar had by then had many liaisons.

Rama took on the job of manager of the health club at the Taj. She regained her youthful vitality and good looks. Since I went to the club every day for exercise and a sauna bath, I became very friendly with her. She even persuaded me to take facial massages which I found deliciously sensuous. Rama had by then resumed some kind of undefined relationship with her first husband.

Johar had a keen eye for publicity. Rama used to visit him once every week. When Johar discovered that she had befriended me, he asked her to bring me over to his apartment in Lotus Court. I was then editing *The Illustrated Weekly of India.* For many months I was a weekly dinner guest in this set-up.

After my sauna bath, Rama and I would proceed to Lotus Court. Rama then rang up Johar who was at the Cricket Club of India playing bridge. She told him to bring some Chinese food from the club restaurant. I played with his miniature Pekingese bitch named Pheeno, the snub nosed. Snub nosed she certainly was, and very cuddlesome. Rama would sometimes open drawers of Johar's bedside table (he always slept on the floor) and pull out stacks of pictures of young girls in bikinis — or less. They were of girls looking for jobs in films. Johar would arrive carrying cartons of Chinese dishes and get out a bottle of premium Scotch for me. Neither he nor Rama touched alcohol. I had my quota of three before we ate dinner. Then Rama dropped me at my apartment and went home. I never got to know where she lived. All I was able to gather was that she had ditched her second husband but I was not sure whether or not she had patched up with Johar. I often pulled her leg about being the only Indian woman I knew who could claim to have two husbands at one time.

Johar sent me the manuscript of his autobiography for serialisation in *The Illustrated Weekly.* It was difficult to tell how much of it was factual, how much the creation of his sick fantasies. In any case, there was more sex in it than was permissible for journals at the time. If Johar was to be believed, he started his sexcapades at the age of twelve. He was spending his vacation with his uncle and aunt who had no children of their own. One night he had (or pretended to have) nightmares and started whimpering in his sleep. His aunt brought him to her bed. He snuggled into her bosom and soon had an erection. He tried to push it into her. She slapped him and told him to behave himself. The next morning he was afraid he would be scolded and sent back home. However, his aunt was sweetness itself. After her husband had left for his office, she offered to bathe him. While she was soaping him, he again got sexually aroused. This time his aunt taught him to what to do with it. It became his daily morning routine. Nevertheless, Johar confessed that in the years of his adolescence what he enjoyed most was being buggered by older boys.

The autobiography did not mention Rama but in the years after their separation he wrote of a starlet (now a star I won't name) whom he set up in a flat in Malabar Hill. Whenever he felt like it, he would drop in on her, have a drink or two and then bed her. One evening he was in a particularly horny mood. When he got to the lady's flat, he was informed by her young Goan maidservant, *"Memsahib bahar gaya"* (madam has gone out). *"Kab ayega?"* (When will she return?) *"Kya maloom? Bahut late hoga."* (I don't know, she will be late), replied the maid. So Johar simply pushed the girl on the bed and mounted her. The girl protested. *"Memsahib ayega to hum boleyga"* (when madam returns, I will tell her), and at the same time opened her legs to her mistress' paramour.

Even more bizarre was his story of how he bedded two sisters and their mother. One sister had been his mistress for some years before she left him to get married. She introduced her younger sister to Johar and asked him to help her get into films. He not only got her a few minor roles but also asked her to stay in his flat. One evening she came back from the studios looking very tired. Johar asked her if she would like a hot cup of tea or something stronger to cheer her up. She replied, "if you really want to know what I would like best, I'd like a nice fuck." The girl left Johar to become a star. Her mother wrote to Johar to thank him for what he had done for her daughters and asked him if she could stay with him for a couple of days when visiting Bombay. One night she came to his bed, stark naked. "I did not want to hurt the old lady's feelings," wrote Johar, and "obliged her the same way I had obliged her daughters."

How could I have published these memoirs without inviting the wrath of the proprietors of the journal on my head?

Johar accused me of cowardice. I accused him of making up stories. The less work he got, the more stories he made up. One day he rang up and asked me to come to his flat with my cameraman. "I am getting engaged to be married later," he told me. "Who to?" I asked him. "To Protima Bedi," he replied. Protima had two grown-up children by Kabir Bedi. She had not yet made a name as an Odissi dancer but gained wide publicity by streaking naked on the sands of Juhu beach. The pictures of her running across without a stitch on her had appeared in many papers. She had a most fetching figure. Johar was at least 30 years older than her, a grandfather in daily communication with his ex-wife, Rama. However, I went along with my photographer. There were dozens of photographers and presspeople present. Johar was dressed in a beige silk *kurta-pajama* with his hair freshly dyed jet black. Protima was decked up in a bridal sari with a lot of gold jewellery on her. With one eye you could see that this was a publicity lark for both of them. The next morning's papers had them on their front pages.

They were back in the news. No marriage followed. Johar talked no more about Protima Bedi.

I had a farewell dinner of sorts before I left Bombay for good. It was like old times. Rama, Pheeno and me with Johar joining us later with Chinese food. By now Pheeno had taken to snuggling in my lap and grunting with contentment. "She seems to be fonder of you than me," remarked Johar, "would you like to take her?" I agreed to accept Pheeno. I would take her with me to Delhi to my family, every one of them passionately fond of animals. When the time came Johar reneged on the promise. "It is like having to give my daughter away, I can't do it," he said by way of explanation. I understood his feelings.

I continued to communicate with Rama long after Johar went out of my life. All said and done I was fonder of her than her ex-husband.

However, I felt a pang of anguish when I read of Johar's death in Bombay. And wondered what became of Pheeno.

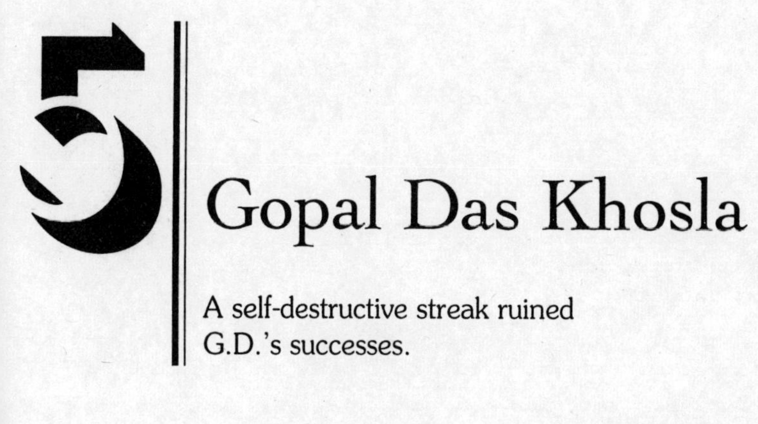

5 Gopal Das Khosla

A self-destructive streak ruined G.D.'s successes.

"I've read your novel Delhi. *I think it is absolutely filthy. I can't think of another word for it except filthy." He may well be right, but he was not the Gopal Das Khosla I knew. He must carry a deep hurt inside him.*

In most cases of married couples I knew, I was friendly with the husband but more often friendlier with the wife. In the case of Gopal Das Khosla and Shakuntala, however, my affections were equally divided between the two. Since they were a close-knit couple, it was not easy for anyone to attach himself or herself to one and exclude the other.

Gopal Das Khosla or G.D. as he was known to his friends was in the ICS. At the time he came into my life we knew the names of all Indians in the ICS posted in our state. They were not many and the few who made it to the heaven-born service were much sought after by parents of nubile daughters and everyone held them in awe as some sort of demigod. They wielded enormous power and patronage.

G.D. had been to school in England before he went to Cambridge University and got into the ICS. He opted to serve in his home state, and unlike most of his contemporaries, chose the judicial over the administrative service. From the vast number of girls from well-to-do Hindu and Sikh families, he chose Shakuntala, one of the daughters of a half-Sikh, half-Hindu family. Her younger sister was likewise picked by another young entrant in the ICS, Kesho Ram. In both cases, the girls had small fortunes to go with their comely faces. G.D. was as pukka a Brown Sahib as I have ever known. Even when posted in remote outlying districts of the Punjab where his home consisted of a couple of tents, he was known to have his *gusal* in a tub, then get into his dinner jacket, have his *aabdaar* to serve him Scotch n' soda before he and his memsahib sat down to their three-course meal of soup, entrée and pudding. Sometime after I had got to know him I asked him if this was true. He replied candidly: "Yes, what's wrong with it?" By the time we became friends, he had discarded the White man's regimen and became more Indianised. His wife and I continued to pull his leg about his earlier sahibish ways.

G.D. rose rapidly in his service. He was clear-headed and had a very good command over the English language. He became a session judge and then a judge of the Lahore High Court, the youngest member of the bench. It was clear to everyone that in due course of time he would become chief justice or make it to the Supreme Court. There were a few other Indians of the ICS on the bench, but the only other probable was Justice A.N. Bhandari who had none of the judicial acumen of Khosla.

Our friendship had an uneasy start. G.D. was a judge; I a practising lawyer. Judges were expected to keep themselves at a respectable distance from members of the bar. G.D. was above these conventions. He was close to Bishen Narain whom he had befriended in England and Bishen's lively, attractive wife Shanti, the only child of the famous revolutionary Lala Hardyal.

He gradually moved towards me and my wife and we started seeing each other in our respective homes. Our wives did not hit it off particularly well. Shakuntala turned out to be somewhat bossy. My wife was always a prickly character more than eager to give anyone tit for tat. I was able to keep peace between the two women by paying exaggerated attention to Shakuntala. She was a large-eyed woman easy on the eye and warmly responsive. After we became close friends many new year eves were spent together drinking and dancing into the early hours.

What drew G.D. towards me was his ambition to become a writer. He was, in fact, keener on literature than on law. Since I had little legal practice I organised a small circle of would-be writers. We met in some home or the other, drank a lot, read our latest compositions of prose or poetry, and applauded each other's efforts. G.D. became the doyen of this mini-literary circle of Lahore.

The partition drove the Khoslas and us out of Lahore. G.D. became the second senior-most judge to Chief Justice A.N. Bhandari of the new High Court of Simla. I happily abandoned the legal profession, got a job with the Ministry of External Affairs and was posted to London. We kept in touch with each other. Whenever I came home on leave or for some assignment, I spent some time with the Khoslas. I spent a few days with them in Simla. There, for the first time, I noted how sparing G.D. was in serving his Scotch. Undoubtedly it was expensive and hard to come by in India and I had got used to drinking duty-free liquor available to diplomats. Some nights I went to bed thirsting for more. But Shakuntala was a generous hostess and good company. G.D.

tried to persuade me to return to the legal profession. The Punjab (then including Haryana and Himachal Pradesh) needed more judges for its High Court. Many jokers had been elevated to the bench. I was no worse than them. However, I refused to be tempted to return to the profession that I had come to loathe with all my heart.

G.D. was one of the panel judges to hear the appeal of Godse and his co-conspirators for the murder of Mahatma Gandhi. I persuaded him to write on the murder case. He did. His book was an instant success, as also his book on the last Mughal emperor Bahadur Shah Zafar. He was very painstaking in his homework. At a dinner party I had for professor T.G.P. Spear, author of a definitive work on the later Mughals, G.D. told him of some factual errors in his book. Professor Spear immediately admitted his errors and promised to correct them in the next reprint.

Close as I was to G.D., I did not detect a streak of vengefulness in him till the couple came to spend a few days with me in Kasauli. He was not getting on with Chief Justice A.N. Bhandari who, despite being a man of mediocre ability, was not above fudging his personal expense accounts.

G.D. compiled them and dictated a note to the Home Minister with a copy to Bhandari. "He will have to answer the charges or resign. He has no other choice," said G.D. to me emphatically. "He has a third choice," I replied. "You can take it from me, he will do neither. He will just keep quiet." That is precisely what Bhandari did. Apart from telling G.D. that it was not a nice thing to do, Bhandari bided his time. The Home Minister did nothing. In the fullness of time Bhandari retired and G.D. became Chief Justice. G.D. was meant for higher positions. However, there was a self-destructive streak in him. This time his writing got him into serious trouble. He started writing a series of short pieces entitled *Grimm's Fairy Tales* after the classic author. They were biting in their sarcasm and most readable. He showed me some before sending them to *The Tribune*.

Unknown to me one of them was defamatory of S.K. Sikri (later Chief Justice of the Supreme Court) and his wife Leela. I did not detect the allusion to the Sikris nor did I know that G.D. was on notoriously bad terms with them. The story was published. Sikri took G.D. to court on charges of libel. I agreed to appear in court on G.D.'s behalf to say that I did not recognise the Sikris in the story. Subsequently G.D. got many assignments from the government and stayed away from India for long periods. But Sikri did not let go of him. Ultimately G.D. had to tender an apology. I suspect that *faux pas* cost him elevation to the Supreme Court.

G.D. has not written anything worthwhile since then. He spends his summers in Kulu-Manali where he has built himself a cottage and his winters in his house in Maharani Bagh, New Delhi. His elder son got into the IAS and the second into the foreign service. The third son became an architect and has a sizeable practice. I barely got to know the youngest, a girl, since I lost touch with the Khoslas quite some time ago.

From being in almost daily contact with them, I have not been with them for some years. The last I saw of G.D. was at the Gymkhana Club annual elections when I found myself standing behind him in the queue of voters. I patted him on the back and said heartily: "G.D. how are you? And how is Shakuntala?" He replied tersely they were all well and added: "I've read your novel *Delhi*. I think it is absolutely filthy. I can't think of another word for it except filthy." He may well be right, but he was not the Gopal Das Khosla I knew. He must carry a deep hurt inside him.

Prem Kirpal

Past experience did not deter Prem Kirpal from making passes at young women.

> *What came as a surprise to me was that Prem, now in his 40s, knew so little about the female sex. One afternoon when overcome by passion he tried to bed her, she pleaded illness and begged him to be patient for a few days.... It was the first time he had heard of women menstruating. "Please don't tell anybody I don't know about this," he begged of me. Of coure I told everyone.*

My friendship with Prem Kirpal has lasted longer than any other–over sixty years. Circumstances threw us together in Lahore, Delhi, London, Paris and back again in Delhi. We happened to be in England at the same time as students: he was in Oxford, I in London. We heard of each other from common friends but never met in those years. It was in Lahore where I settled down to practise law and he got a job as a lecturer in Dayal Singh College that we got to know each other. His father, Ishwar Das, was then Deputy Registrar and later Registrar of the

Punjab University. They were Sahajdhati Sikhs. Prem's mother came from a family of orthodox Khalsas. Ishwar Das was much influenced by leaders of the Singh Sabha movement, the poet Bhai Veer Singh, Dr. Jodh Singh and the Attatiwala family. This was a common link between his family and my wife's parents who were ardent followers of Bhai Veer Singh. It did not take us long to start visiting each other's homes.

Prem was very conscious of having been a student of Balliol College, Oxford, and always wore his college tie. In his scheme of things Oxford was the best university in the world, Balliol the best college in Oxford and he privileged to be the product of the best institution. An anecdote told about him was that when leaving Oxford to catch his boat to return to India he happened to be having his breakfast in the dining car of the Oxford-London train. Sitting across the table was an Englishman likewise having breakfast. Over the din and rattle of the train he asked Prem, "Would you mind passing me the salt?" Prem promptly held up his college tie and replied, "Yes, this is a Balliol tie."

Soon I found out other connections with the Kirpal family. All the sons had been to Government College: Amar Nath, Prem, Pritam and Prakash. Amar Nath was a lawyer and edited a law journal. His one-year-old son Bhupinder (Cuckoo) also became a lawyer, then judge of the Delhi High Court and is now Chief Justice of the Gujarat High Court. Pritam who played hockey for the college retired from the army as a general. Prakash became a draftsman in the Survey of India in Dehradun. There were also three or four sisters of whom two, Sita and Leela, were then unmarried. Ishwar Das often used to boast of the virility of the Kirpals when he rued that Prem had not found a wife and kept up the family tradition of fecundity.

Actually Prem was very eager to find a mate. His first choice was his closest friend Mangat Rai's elder sister. Priobala was then teaching in Kinnaird College. Prem started calling on her. He was not a man of many words, and when it came to women even less vocal. He was not getting anywhere because in Kinnaird College there were always some women about. At my suggestion he persuaded Priobala to come out with him for a drive. He did not have a car and could not afford a taxi. So he hired a tonga and the two went around Lawrence Gardens and other beauty spots of Lahore. He was still not getting anywhere. I told him that some women responded to action and he should simply grab her in his arms and kiss her. He decided to give it a try. The next time he took Priobala for a tonga ride he told her: "Prio, you know what Khushwant asked me to do? He said I should take you in my arms and kiss you." Priobala was incensed. "He is an absolute rascal. You can tell him that from me," she added. Prem told me. That was to remain the pattern of Prem's many romances.

After partition we found ourselves in Delhi and then London. He was education officer, I a press attaché. Our boss Krishna Menon did not like Prem but liked me to start with. Prem was sent back to the ministry. A couple of years later, I resigned my job and was back in Delhi. We resumed our friendship. Prem was a Joint Secretary and an eligible bachelor. One afternoon while sharing the office car with a lady colleague his hand slipped and fell on her shoulder. The lady promptly responded by giving him a full-blooded kiss on his lips. There was no escape. His father approved of the girl (she was South Indian); their engagement was announced. What came as a surprise to me was that Prem, now in his 40s, knew so little about the female sex. One afternoon when overcome by passion he tried to bed her; she pleaded illness and begged him to be patient for a few days. But Prem's passions had been aroused to a feverish pitch and he saw with his own eyes blood between her thighs. He confided the discovery to me. It was the first time he had heard of women menstruating. "Please don't tell anybody I don't know about this," he begged of me. Of course, I told everyone. The way he broke with the lady was even more amusing. She fixed the date for their wedding. Prem disappeared from Delhi and sent her a telegram saying he had broken his leg and the marriage would have to be postponed indefinitely. For a few days he even had his leg put in plaster.

Past experiences did not deter Prem from making passes at young women. And when they responded, he beat a hasty retreat.

What I have said about Prem may make him appear very light-weight. He was not. He became head of the Cultural Division of UNESCO, Member and then Chairman of the Executive Board. Although he knew very little of art or music either Eastern or Western he made an excellent chairman and conducted meetings with great skill. His strength lay in gentleness and offending nobody. Although I made cruel fun of him he remained devoted to my entire family. We travelled together all over Europe and Latin America. My accounts of these journeys are peppered with anecdotes about Prem. Once in Madrid I had to bully him to visit Prado by telling him that it had a richer collection than the Louvre and his colleagues were bound to ask him about it. He strode through the Prado galleries in fifteen minutes flat. Back in Paris he told his friends that he thought Prado was better than the Louvre. They were horrified and told him so. He, in turn, was angry with me for having exaggerated the quality of Prado.

At another time, still in Madrid, we decided to invite Elizabeth Adiseshiah, who was staying in another hotel with her husband Malcolm, for dinner, as her husband was busy in a conference. Prem went to call up from the hotel telephone in the lobby which was packed with guests having tea. When he got her on the line Prem began to shout at the top of his voice: "Lisbeth, this is Prem. If you are not doing anything this evening then come and have dinner with us." Everyone in the lobby stopped talking to listen to the announcement. When he came back he told me, "Elizabeth will come for dinner." I replied, "I know, so does everyone else in the hotel. Why did you have to shout so loudly?" His reply was classic: "She is in the other hotel which is long distance from here."

Prem returned to Delhi to become Secretary of the Ministry of Education. He had a strong patron in Dr. S. Radhakrishnan who saw to it that Prem got what he wanted. Prem was not averse to laying on flattery when it was required. "You are the greatest philosopher in the world today," he told Radhakrishnan. I could not resist cutting in, "Sir, he has not read even one of your books." Prem gracefully acknowledged: "That is true. I have not read your books but everyone tells me you are a great philosopher. I accept that." Prem who knew little about Radhakrishnan's works remained his favourite. I who had read almost everything he had written was kept at a distance.

After retirement from government service Prem took on Delhi Public Schools — perhaps the largest chain of schools in the country. He got me nominated to the board as he needed support against mischief-makers who were forever trying to take over the management. Although DPS kept him busy, he still had a lot of time on his hands. He has evolved a new pattern of living. He gets up late. Then he takes a long walk in the Lodhi Gardens. After lunch he takes a long siesta before tea. He is in the India International Centre almost every evening. Back home, he has yet another bout in bed. By dinner time he is fresher than anyone else. He cannot bear to be alone because he does not read — he has the largest unread library in his house. He invites the same people for his dinner parties. And if he cannot get anyone, he lands up in my flat with the announcement "what's happening?" And then he stays on for dinner.

Prem has become hard of hearing. He has also taken to painting in the most garish of colours. The walls of his sitting and dining room are plastered with his paintings (one was made an emblem for a T-shirt). He also composes poetry at the drop of a hat.

He has an ardent admirer in Santosh Jain who periodically organises exhibitions of his paintings and functions to release his latest collection of poems.

He loves to celebrate his birthdays when he keeps an open house. Champagne and Scotch flow. On the central table he keeps albums. One has pictures of the women he admired or loved. This starts with Indira Gandhi, goes on to my wife, Kamala Chaudhary, Sita Chari, Kapila Vatsyayan, Romilla Thapar, Reba Shome, Cedra Castellaine, Rayonde Sokolovsky, Inge Fisher, Trude and a host of others I don't know. The other is of himself with notables like Dr. Radhakrishnan and Director General of UNESCO. Besides these albums is the latest edition of the Balliol College magazine.

Prem is now 85. He composed a poem for the occasion entitled "Four Score and Five":

Four Score and Five
Brings sweet memories to Mind
In the passage of my time
From Joy and Peace of Mind
To the Maturing of Delight
Basked in Love and Light
Toward the close of Life!
To Four Score and Five
At this Celebration of Life
And gaily marching time
I raise a Toast tonight

In thankfulness to Life
For its gifts of great delight!
Four Score and Five
Brood and sing in passing time
Many memories of Life
Forays of Love and Light
Quest of Spirit's heights
Dreams of great delight
In flights of Heart and Mind!

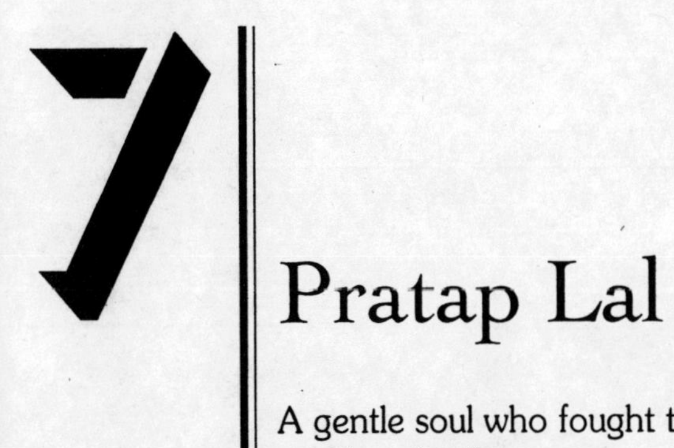

7 Pratap Lal

A gentle soul who fought the toughest battles.

Then I saw a few letters he wrote to my fiancée who had joined a college in London, warning her against the hazards of marrying a Sikh. In those letters he had made cartoons depicting me without my turban and my beard hanging down to my navel. They were very funny and extremely well drawn.

There is a Hindustani saying that men of destiny have signs of greatness even in their infancy. No one who knew Pratap Lal in school and college spotted any such tell-tale signs indicating the heights to which he would rise. We became friends at Modern School when we were only five years old.

Ten years later, we exchanged turbans to become *Dharambhais* — brothers in faith. There was nothing *dharmic* about my intentions; though only 15, I was besotted by Pratap's sister, Roma, who was two years older than me.

The Lals were a mixed Punjabi, Bengali family. Pratap's father Rai Bahadur Basant Lal, Assistant Commissioner of

Income-tax was a Punjabi. His mother was a Bengali Sarkar who spoke Punjabi fluently. In their home they spoke four languages with equal fluency: English, Hindustani, Bengali and Punjabi. They were Brahmos and more liberal in their views than most Indian families of Delhi. Roma was the heartthrob of my generation.

Pratap, though he managed to pass his exams, was a poor student. He had a strong aversion to sports of any kind. The only thing that made him different from other boys of his age was his consuming interest in aeroplanes. At the age of 15, he joined the Delhi Flying Club and became the youngest man to get a licence to fly solo.

His college years were as undistinguished as his school record.

In 1935 he joined me again in Kings College, London, and enrolled for the Bar at one of the Inns of Court. We spent a vacation together cycling all over England and Wales. At an inn near Tintern Abbey, where we spent a night, he was very pleased to learn that the inn-keeper had taken him to be my son.

An aspect of Pratap's hidden talents was revealed to me during his early years in England. Unbeknown to me he wrote articles on some of his experiences in the country. They were published in the *Manchester Guardian*, then the most prestigious journal in the country.

No Indian student in England had ever succeeded in getting published. Then I saw a few letters he wrote to my fiancée who had joined a college in London, warning her against the hazards of marrying a Sikh. In those letters he had made cartoons depicting me without my turban and my beard hanging down to my navel. They were very funny and extremely well drawn.

The outbreak of the war in 1939 rescued Pratap Lal from what might well have been an undistinguished career at the

Bar. He promptly threw away his law books and joined the Air Force.

Being familiar with the workings of aircraft he had no problem rising rapidly up the ranks. And displayed yet another unknown characteristic: bravery.

He flew dive bombers supporting General Slim's drive against the Japanese in Burma. He was mentioned in despatches and awarded the Distinguished Flying Cross. When independence came he held the rank of Squadron Leader. He was chosen for an advanced course in Andover and was the first pilot of the IAF to fly faster than the speed of sound.

When I was Krishna Menon's PRO in London, Pratap came there as head of a team to purchase fighter aircraft. Menon had his own middleman hawking machines which would give them highest commissions.

Lal inspected the machines and turned them down. Menon was furious and accused Lal of accepting bribes from rival dealers. Pratap stood his ground and earned Menon's hatred. When Menon was made the Defence Minister he made no secret of his dislike for Lal.

There were others, notably J.R.D. Tata who knew Lal's worth. In 1957, he was made general manager of the Indian Airlines Corporation, a post he held for five years till Menon was fired from defence ministership following our defeat at the hands of the Chinese. Pratap Lal was back in the Indian Air Force. He fought the 1965 Indo-Pak war and was given a Padma Bhushan.

In 1966 he was made managing director of the Hindustan Aeronautics Ltd. factory at Bangalore. My wife and I spent some days with him and his wife Ela (Hashi). They were an abstemious couple. He did not smoke or drink. We had to extort our quota of Scotch from him every evening. He was also very prudish. No talk of nudity or sex. No dirty jokes.

In 1969 Pratap became Air Chief Marshal, with a Padma Vibhushan added to his many Air Force decorations. He masterminded the Air Force operations in the 1971 war against Pakistan over the liberation of Bangladesh.

It was his strategy which knocked the Pakistani Air Force out of the eastern skies and made the advance of our land forces to Dhaka into a kind of walk-over. Two years later he retired to live an almost isolated life with his family. He died in London on August 13, 1982. I was present at his cremation the next day in the Delhi electric crematorium. So ended a friendship that had lasted over half a century.

Shakespeare's lines from *Julius Caeser* are the most fitting tribute I could pay to my departed friend:

His life was gentle.
And the elements so mixed in him
That nature itself would stand up and say
  to all the world: This was a Man.

A.G. Noorani

The most charming side of Noorani was his naïveté when it came to women.

He tried to imitate the Jinnah approach to problems, analysing their pros and cons with cold logic and expounding them in measured tones.... The difference between them was that though he kept aloof from others, Jinnah was courteous towards everyone he met. Noorani, on the other hand, could get into angry arguments with his clients, solicitors and judges.

"If you ever write about me, I will never speak to you again," said Ghafoor Noorani to me soon after we got to know each other in Bombay. Since he stopped talking to me soon after, it makes no difference to me now.

I had read many articles written by him and was eager to get him to write for *The Illustrated Weekly of India* of which I had just been appointed editor (1969). He dealt with serious subjects like the Constitution, corruption in high places, Muslim Personal Law, etc. Though he had no turn of phrase or wit, what he wrote was well documented, authentic and thought-provoking. Apparently he was equally eager to write for the *Weekly* which was fast picking up circulation.

The introduction was made by my assistant editor, Fatma Zakaria, to whom he was distantly related. Both were Cutchi Memons born and brought up in Bombay.

"I have only two interests in my life," Noorani told me soon after we got to know each other, "*Vakalat aur siyasat* — law and politics." However, it was neither in one or the other that Noorani earned fame. It was *sihaafat* — journalism — that made him a household word throughout India.

Though *vakalat*, *siyasat* and *sihaafat* were his main pre-occupations, after a while when he opened up with me I discovered that he was also interested in Urdu poetry, had a sizeable repertoire of verse including the bawdy and was not averse to paying attention to the fair sex.

Noorani was and remains a bachelor. He lived (and still lives) in a one bedroom apartment close to Kemp's Corner on Malabar Hill. Although he had a good cook, he liked to dine out if he found pleasant company. He wasn't a party man and preferred being with just one other person.

I was then leading a bachelor existence living as a paying guest with a young Parsi couple who only gave me breakfast. I had to go to restaurants for my evening meal. Soon we began to meet every evening, and take a walk along Marine Drive to Nariman Point. We had coconut juice and came to my room in Churchgate. I had my Scotch while he sipped orange juice or whatever non-alcoholic drink I had to offer. Then we went to restaurants in and around Churchgate or Colaba.

After our meal we went to our favourite *paanwallah*. Noorani's instructions were precise which he rattled off in one breath: *kaatha-choona-supari-masala*. Then we took leave of each other. He took a taxi to Kemp's Corner; I walked home to my *pension*.

I found Noorani very good company because he was very well informed on current affairs and very clear-headed. I could see that he took M.A. Jinnah as his role model. He invariably wore a suit and tie, socks and shoes even on the warmest of summer days.

Before stepping out, he would examine his appearance in my bathroom mirror, brush back his well-oiled hair with both his hands till he was assured that what he saw in the mirror met his approval.

He tried to imitate the Jinnah approach to problems, analysing their pros and cons with cold logic and expounding them in measured tones. However, while Jinnah rose to the top in law and politics, Noorani, who probably had as sound a grasp of law as Jinnah, had a modest practice and made no mark in politics. The difference between them was that though he kept aloof from others, Jinnah was courteous towards everyone he met. Noorani, on the other hand, could get into angry arguments with his clients, solicitors and judges.

He had a knack for needling people to the point of exasperation. I was told that once he riled a fellow lawyer to such an extent that the other simply picked up Noorani and dumped him out of the window.

Many common friends who saw us together every evening told me, "It won't last very long, Noorani is a compulsive quarreller. One day he will drop you as he has dropped all his other friends."

Our friendship lasted longer than anticipated by people who knew Noorani better than I. We were together in many seminars: Delhi, Hyderabad, Goa and Islamabad. Noorani's contribution was usually the most lucid of any presented by other participants.

He was a little uneasy in Pakistan: he had been detained during the Indo-Pak war for having pro-Pak sympathies. That was a calumny perpetrated by our government against many Indian Muslims.

In Islamabad Noorani put the Indian point of view with much stronger emphasis than any of the other Indians. But the Pakistanis would not take anything said by an Indian Muslim seriously. I do not think Noorani was happy with the reception he got.

After months of keeping company with me, the very proper and correct Noorani began to let down his hair occasionally and bandy bawdy Urdu verse with me.

This was most unusual for a man who was known to snub people who took the liberty of calling him by his first name Ghafoor; "I don't think you know me well enough to call me Ghafoor. I am A.G. Noorani to you."

The most charming side of Noorani was his naïveté when it came to women. Once we were entertaining two girls who had arrived that evening in Bombay. One was a six-foot tall Canadian, the other a petite American. After dinner we walked them to their hotel. The tall girl and I were ahead, Noorani and the petite American girl following a few steps behind us.

After we had bidden them good night, Noorani and I walked on towards Nariman Point. He was very excited. "*Yaar,* you know what that American girl said to me? When I asked her if she was single or married, she replied, 'I am married but I commit adultery.' What do you think of that? Doesn't it amount to an invitation?"

"No," I told him. "I know many American girls. They say that kind of thing without meaning anything."

Noorani refused to accept my explanation and tried to date the girl. She refused his invitation and later rang up. "Please tell your friend to get off my back."

I asked her if she had really told Noorani that she committed adultery. The American girl replied, "Yes, I did. And I do. But I didn't mean to commit it with your friend."

Noorani was a sentimental kind of a chap. Once he was taken up by an English woman, a mousy nondescript girl who had very little to say for herself. He persuaded her to come to my room for a drink and then come out for dinner with us.

While Noorani and I were having our drinks (his being a lemonade) my phone rang. It was the English girl. She begged me to be excused because she was feeling unwell. She imitated a very sick person's voice.

I broke the news to Noorani. The high spirits he came with went into a steep decline. He wanted to get over with dinner and go home.

We went to a restaurant in Churchgate. As I entered I saw the same girl sitting with Bhai Chand Patel, then a lawyer-cum-journalist whom Noorani loathed.

I turned back and took Noorani with me to another restaurant. He was out of sorts throughout the meal. I don't know what he had to say to the girl. There were many such episodes all with equally unromantic endings.

Why Noorani did not have an arranged marriage with a nice Cutchi Memon girl, I was never able to find out. He was eminently eligible. He earned good money and had become an all-India celebrity.

One time some friend did try to arrange a meeting between him and an equally celebrated Muslim lady journalist. They were to meet in a hotel in Delhi. The hotel had five restaurants. It was not specified where the tryst was to take place. The lady waited in one restaurant, Noorani in another.

After half-an-hour both decided to call it a day. As fate would have it, they found themselves in the same elevator. Without ever having met before they recognised each other. Noorani held up his wrist watch and pointed to the time. He deliberately mispronounced the lady's name and said with some anger, "You see the time? I wasted half-an-hour waiting for you. I am a busy man, you know?"

Not to be outdone, the lady showed him her wrist watch, told him how her name was pronounced and remarked, "I too have wasted my time and am as busy as you are."

They began to wrangle in the lift and carried on to do so in the lobby till they got to their respective cars. This is as close as I know Noorani came to finding a life-companion.

Noorani was, and probably is today, a very touchy and cantankerous person. It is hard to believe that he dropped me because I did not answer his telephone call. He never tried to find out whether or not I had received his message; nor if I had tried to get him on the line and failed. An unanswered telephone call he regarded as an act of gross discourtesy deserving to be punished with *kuttee* — severance of relationship.

I am not the only one whom he befriended and then cast off like a worn-out garment. I know dozens of others who met the same fate. A.G. Noorani has innumerable admirers but no friends.

9 Rajni Patel

A little drunk, Rajni Patel married Bakul and then promptly burst into tears.

He was in turns warm and generous, in turns cold and utterly callous. I had some affection for him but little respect because he was totally amoral. I hope that he died a fulfilled man with an easy conscience.

My first few meetings with Rajni Patel were in railway trains. Both of us were studying law; he in Cambridge, I in London. We were also at the Inns of Court where dining a few nights during term time was compulsory. Rajni came down from Cambridge to attend dinner at his Inn. I came from Welwyn Garden City where I lived. We found ourselves catching the same train from Kings' Cross station. Welwyn was half way to Cambridge. At times we were joined by Mohan Kumaramangalam (later cabinet minister in Mrs. Indira Gandhi's Government) who was also studying law in Cambridge and the Inns of Court. We were often in the same compartment.

At that time I was a teetotaller and did not touch the bottles placed on our tables. Rajni and Kumaramangalam helped themselves liberally to wines that were offered free of charge. By the time they boarded the train, they were usually in high spirits. Both were leftists, probably card-holding members of the Communist Party. It did not take much for us to get into arguments. I recall that on one occasion the debate got so heated that Rajni gestured to Kumaramangalam and said: "Let's throw this fellow out of the train."

Our last encounter in Europe was one summer when I was going to Paris for my vacations. Rajni and Krishna Menon happened to be on the same train bound for some international conference. They did not take much notice of me as they were deeply engrossed in discussing resolutions they meant to put forward. At Dover where we had to detrain to get on the ferry to take us across the English Channel there was a long queue at the immigration counter. I took my place at the end of the queue. Menon took Rajni by the hand and marched ahead. The immigration officer told them to get back in the line. Menon lost his temper and accused the official of racial prejudice. The bewildered White man did not want to get into an argument. He simply stamped their passports and told them to fuck off.

Back home in India, I kept hearing of Rajni's climb to fame in the legal profession and in party politics. He had become a formidable figure in Bombay's leftist trade union circles and commanded a large legal practice. He, along with like-minded Russi Karanjia, editor of *Blitz,* and Ramesh Sanghvi, threw all their weight behind Krishna Menon to see him elected to Parliament instead of Acharya Kripalani. I could not understand these three characters all of whom professed to be ardent socialists fighting the cause of poor workers, while all the three lived in a style which would be the envy of a rich capitalist.

Russi Karanjia had no qualms about backing the winning side. He was pro-Arab and anti-Israeli; also the Shah of Iran's chief spokesman in India. He also gave wide publicity to

Godmen particularly Sai Baba. Ramesh Sanghvi went one step further. While preaching communism to his countrymen he worked as the Shah's PRO in Tehran and London. He was the greatest name dropper I had met. I had lost track of Rajni but when I moved to Bombay in 1969 I did not particularly want to cultivate his friendship. The few times we met, we shook hands and parted saying: "We must meet again."

We did not see much of each other till Rajni was nominated member of the Board of Bennett Coleman and Company which owned *The Times of India* group of papers and magazines including *The Illustrated Weekly of India* of which I was editor. Rajni had by then become a great favourite of Mrs. Gandhi and her principal fund collector in Bombay. Politicians, industrialists and civil servants fawned over him. Among his closer friends were Rafiq Zakaria and his wife Fatma who was my assistant editor. We started seeing each other at dinner parties. Rajni drew closer to me than his other friends. When the Zakarias sponsored my name for the award of Padma Bhushan, Rajni saw it through the Prime Minister's office. The one quality Rajni had which few politicians have was that he never made false promises.

At that time Rajni had divorced his wife Bakul, who had given him two sons and was living with a divorcee. I was often invited to their flat for dinner. Once he had me invited to the house of Dr. Banerjee of Sandoz to discuss plans to raise funds for the relief of the famine-stricken in Maharashtra. Many top industrialists were present. French champagne, premium Scotch and vintage wines were served before and with the meal. I made some caustic remark about it being the right atmosphere to talk about the sufferings of the hungry. My irony did not impress any of those present. Least of all Rajni who believed in good living.

Despite enjoying Rajni's lavish hospitality and patronage, I never really got to know him as a human being. He obviously earned a great deal of money; it was not through legal practice but through getting things done for his clients for a fat fee. He mulcted the rich of Bombay in the name of Mrs. Gandhi and the Congress Party: how much of the collection went to the party's secret funds, to Mrs. Gandhi or was kept by him, no one really knew. Mrs. Gandhi was happy with the arrangement; her son Sanjay was not and accused Rajni of fudging accounts. There were people who accused him of all kinds of double dealing. K.K. Shah went to the extent of accusing Rajni of contriving a plane crash in which his son was killed. I was never able to confront Rajni with these accusations as I did not enjoy his confidence. I was not even sure of his relationship with Bakul. She was a homely looking, self-effacing type ever eager to please Rajni and his friends. Rajni was also known to have affairs with other women. Protima Bedi later published a few love letters exchanged between them.

It took a long time for Rajni to make up his mind to marry Bakul. I was not in Bombay at the time but got the details from people who were present. It was at a dinner party where more than usual quantities of Scotch were consumed. Rajni was a heavy drinker; he drank more than his evening quota. Then somebody suggested that he marry Bakul. He nodded assent. Immediately someone in the party (I believe it was Mota Chudasama) went out at midnight to get a pandit to perfom the ceremony. I was told that Rajni's first reaction on getting married was to burst into tears. Whether they were tears of regret or joy, no one could tell.

On my return to Bombay, I went to felicitate the Patels. It was a new Bakul I met: radiant and self-confident. A simple ceremony had changed her from a self-conscious and reticent mistress to the wife of the most powerful man in Bombay.

Not long after the marriage one of Rajni's sons from his first marriage was involved in a car crash and suffered serious head injuries. He was taken to the hospital in a coma and remained unconscious for almost a month. The hospital became a place of pilgrimage for politicians and civil servants: governors, chief ministers, cabinet ministers, all called on the Patels to register their concern.

Rajni had a room booked on the ground floor of the hospital to receive visitors. It was connected by an intercom with the room where the boy lay unconscious attended by two nurses. I was also expected to call. I did. On my second visit to the hospital I saw an extremely attractive middle-aged woman sitting on a stool beside the lift. As she saw me come in she stood up to greet me. "I am Rajni Patel's first wife. My son is lying unconscious on the fifth floor. I am not allowed to see him. I am his mother." I was taken aback. She was beautiful but cold as ice. I mumbled something in sympathy and promised to have a word with Rajni. I suspect it was Bakul and not Rajni who had banned the mother's access to her child. In the crowded reception room where tea, coffee and snacks were being served (Rajni kept some Scotch for me in the cupboard) I took Rajni aside and told him of his first wife's ordeal. He fixed me with a steely gaze and replied: "You keep out of this business." It was not Bakul but Rajni who had ordered the hospital staff not to allow his first wife access to her son.

What kind of a man was Rajni Patel? In turns warm and generous, in turns cold and utterly callous. I had some affection for him but little respect because he was totally amoral. I hope that he died a fulfilled man with an easy conscience. After his death Bakul claimed that he had left her penniless. There was certainly no truth in that. Apart from his two spacious flats (and I am sure he left more real estate and cash) she probably has the best private collection of M.F. Hussain and other contemporary Indian painters. She is the most elegantly dressed and bejewelled lady in the metropolis of Bombay. Bakul remains as much of an enigma for me as was her husband Rajni.

[illegible] of the [illegible] [illegible]. The [illegible]
[illegible] for [illegible] and [illegible]
[illegible]
[illegible] together [illegible]
[illegible] on the [illegible]
[illegible]
with [illegible]
two [illegible]
[illegible]
[illegible] she [illegible]
[illegible]
[illegible]
[illegible] see [illegible]
She was [illegible]
[illegible]
[illegible] who had [illegible]
[illegible]
[illegible]
[illegible]
[illegible]
[illegible]
[illegible]
[illegible]
[illegible]
[illegible]
[illegible]
[illegible]
[illegible] had [illegible]
[illegible]
[illegible]
[illegible]
[illegible]
[illegible]
[illegible]
[illegible]

10

Manzur Qadir

Will Manzur Qadir approve of this?

He also composed bawdy verse and recited it with great gusto to a purely male audience. He was extremely proper and prudish in the company of women.

Whenever anyone asks me "Who was the person you admired most and who influenced your way of thinking?" I answer without hesitation — "Manzur Qadir."

Not many people in India would have heard the name of Manzur Qadir.

Even in Pakistan, where he was born and is buried, most people will have heard of him as an eminent lawyer who was made Foreign Minister by President Ayub Khan and then Chief Justice of the Supreme Court. Only a small group of friends knew him as a human being. I was among those handful who had the privilege of being his closest friend in the years we lived in Lahore. Our friendship continued after partition. He took over my house, had all my books, furniture, and even empty bottles of whisky sent to me. At considerable risk to his life, he dropped my Sikh servant across the border when intercommunal strife was at its worst.

Since our children were about the same age and went to college in England at the same time, the close association between the families continued. Manzur died some 15 years ago in London.

Whenever I visit Lahore, one of my top assignments is to visit his grave, strew rose petals on it, recite the *fatiha* (he, like me, was an agnostic), and shed some tears.

Manzur was a short, bald, beady-eyed man. He was by no means handsome and yet men and women were drawn towards him like moths towards a flame.

Though he was an average student in school and college, within four years of starting practice in Lyallpur, he was acknowledged as the most up and coming lawyer in Punjab. By the time he shifted to Lahore to practise at the High Court, he was recognised as the best lawyer in the bar. He was as fluent in English as he was in Urdu. Though born a Punjabi, he avoided speaking the language. He had a passion for Urdu poetry and could reel off Iqbal by the hour. He also composed bawdy verse and recited it with great gusto to purely male audience. He was extremely proper and prudish in the company of women. He did not have any hang-ups about food or drink — he was a teetotaller and relished fruit. During winter months he would eat Malta oranges by the dozen, splitting each with his bare hands; in summers he thought nothing of demolishing six mangoes at a sitting. He was a chain smoker. The only relaxation he knew was going to the cinema.

What was so great about Manzur Qadir? Two things: he never said a hurtful thing about anyone. And he never told a lie. Within a short time he became a kind of touchstone to judge the rights and wrongs of every course of action. We would often ask ourselves: "Will Manzur approve of this?" Such combination of ability, integrity, consideration and kindness, I have never found in any other human being.

11 Bharat Ram

Bharat was generous by instinct and kept an open house.

Bharat was outgoing; liked being among friends and beautiful women... He also became addicted to golf and spent long hours on fairways and greens.... He liked his drink and became a chain smoker, burning away upwards of eighty cigarettes a day.

Sometime in the early 1920s, two young *Bania* boys joined Modern School, New Delhi. They became the butts of pranks by their schoolmates for the simple reason that they had long *chuttiyas* or *bodees* (pigtails) dangling down from the top of their heads to the back of their necks. They tied a part of them in knots. Though some very young Sikh boys wore long hair plaited like girls, we had got used to them but *bodees* were something new to Modern School. Boys would tug at them and run away. The two brothers' lives were made thoroughly miserable but they did not have the courage to snip their pigtails off for fear of their orthodox parents.

One day some boys stuck chewing gum in their pigtails. Much as they tried to get it out by disentangling their hair and washing it with soap, the gum stuck. In sheer desperation they cut off their *chuttiyas*. Their days of torture were over. The brothers were Bharat Ram and Charat Ram, sons of the richest man in Delhi, Shri Ram, owner of the Delhi Cloth Mills. To us they were known as Bharato and Charato.

I was a year senior to Bharat. He was in the same class as a girl named Kaval Malik who was later destined to become my wife. Bharat, like many other Modern School boys, was enamoured of her, and as they grew into adolescence, their admiration turned into adoration. Kaval Malik was a very pretty girl, somewhat tomboyish; she cycled to school and played hockey and football with the boys. She grew into a beautiful young lady. My acquaintance with Bharat would have ended when I passed out of school. It continues to this day because Bharat, his father Sir Shri Ram, and his wife Shiela continued to cherish my wife's friendship and perforce had to suffer mine.

Bharat and Charat were indifferent to their studies. But Bharat, despite his small size, turned out to be the best hockey, football and cricket player of the school. He played centre-forward in our hockey team and was not daunted by the opposing side's full backs trying to hit him in his shins. He was our top goal scorer.

Bharat was put into the family business immediately after he passed out of college. I realised pretty early in life that true friendship can exist only among equals in wealth and status. Bharat was the son of a very wealthy man and attracted sycophants and self-seekers like flies to a pot of honey. Some pretended to be rude and to speak their minds to him. Bharat was unable to see through the game. He was generous by instinct and kept an open house for everyone. He was very keen on bridge and lost heavily at every session which went on almost non-stop over weekends. The only use

I made of him was to spend summer evenings bathing in his private pool.

When I was commissioned by Charat to write a biography of his father, I discovered how Bharat came to marry Shiela. Sir Shri Ram put an ad in the matrimonial columns of *The Hindustan Times* for a suitable bride for his son. Shri Ram's standing as an industrialist brought in a large number of applications, among them one from Shiela's parents. Father and son went to inspect the girl. By then Shiela had got so fed up of being periodically put up for show and made to sing for parents of eligible sons that she refused to deck herself up and appeared before Shri Ram and his son in a soiled, crushed sari she was wearing. Other suitors had found her too dark. Bharat had no hesitation in saying "yes."

They were duly married and she gave Bharat four strapping sons. One of them was born about the same time as my son, Rahul. That summer Shiela, Bharat and the child came to spend some days with us in Mashobra near Simla. Shiela was unable to feed her son. My wife, who was better endowed, had the two boys suckling her. Thereafter, Sir Shri Ram always presented her with a saree on his grandson's birthday and treated her like his own *bahu*.

The atmosphere in the Shri Ram household was very formal. Attendance at lunches was understood to be compulsory. Like a patriarch, Shri Ram sat at the head of the table and took note of any one of the family who was absent. He enquired about their health and if they were not ill and still missing for more than a couple of days, he dictated a note to his secretary and had it delivered to the defaulter, asking for an explanation. Whenever tensions built up in the family, they were diffused by an exchange of correspondence between people living under the same roof. The only one allowed to talk loudly was the patriarch. Others spoke in whispers. Lady Shri Ram rarely, if ever, appeared in the family gatherings. She always wore a soiled white sari and had an obsession that she could not afford to buy a new one.

Shri Ram was a man of strong likes and dislikes. Those he liked would live off him endlessly. One couple was Dr. Kapur and his wife who were his guests right from the time they migrated from Lahore in 1947 till he died. He had a soft spot for Susheila Rani and gave her husband Babu Rao Patel, editor of *Mother India*, money to buy jeeps to fight his election. He paid for their air fare Bombay-Delhi-Bombay whenever they wanted to come to Delhi. To start with, he was very fond of his daughter-in-law, Shiela, and shamelessly kissed her on her lips when she came to touch his feet. Then for no rhyme or reason he developed a strong aversion to her. She was very hurt and turned sour against him. He liked my wife but did not think I was worthy of being her husband. Whenever I met him sitting on the lawn in front of his house, he asked, "*Kuchh kaam-vaam bhee karta hai ya baap kee kamai par rahta hai*?" (Do you do any kind of work or do you live off your father's bounty?) I avoided meeting him.

Bharat and Shiela, though they had four sons, had very little else in common with each other. He was generous and reckless in spending money on his friends. She was tight-fisted and resented his recklessness. She was gifted and under the tutelage of Pandit Ravi Shankar, had learnt to play the sitar like a professional. Her eldest son Vinay turned out to be a noted singer of classical Hindustani music. Bharat, though he admired these talents in his wife and son, did little to project them. Bharat was outgoing, liked being among friends and beautiful women. Shiela was withdrawn and resented her husband paying attention to other women. Bharat also became addicted to golf and spent long hours on fairways and greens. He became a first class golf player and patron-in-chief of the Delhi Golf Club. He liked his drink, and became a chain smoker, burning away upwards of eighty cigarettes a day. They began to drift apart. Shiela became a Radha Soami and began to spend many months of the year at the ashram in Beas. The arrangement ended the bickerings at home and both were at peace with themselves.

Once Shiela and Bharat came to stay with us in Paris where I was working with UNESCO. I had a small house in a suburb called Bourg La Reine. We had one spare bedroom and a living-in English maid. Shiela was coming from Moscow where she had gone with an Indian women's delegation. Bharat was in England playing some golf tournament. They were to meet in Paris to return home to Delhi. I did my best to dissuade them from staying with us and suggested they would be far more comfortable in a hotel. But Shiela would not hear of it. "I have had enough of hotels. I will stay with you. I can help in washing dishes and sweeping the floors," she wrote. I picked her up at the airport and brought her home. Bharat was to arrive the same evening. Instead of him there was a telegram from him saying he had been delayed on business and would come a couple of days later. Sheila was very upset. She asked me if she could make a call to England. Instead of ringing up the hotel where Bharat was staying, she rang up the country home of a couple Bharat was friendly with. It was Bharat's misfortune that he picked up the phone. Sheila gave him a tongue-lashing. It went on and on. My nerves were frayed. My wife and I decided to stroll outside and let Sheila get rid of her anger.

We returned after half an hour. Sheila was still on the phone. At the time, calls from France to England were double the rate than calls from England to France. When she had finished, Sheila said to me, "I would like to pay for the call but I know you won't let your sister pay for it." The brother-sister business cost me dearly. She saw some old Mughal miniatures in our sitting room. She picked up the best and said, "*Agar tu mera bhai hai to yeh mujhey dey dey*" (If you are my brother, you give this to me). She had a much larger and better collection of rare paintings in her home in Delhi and I hoped she would let me take one of them in return. In Delhi I told her, "Shiela, this can't be a one-way traffic. You took the best I had. You let me pick the one I like in your collection." Shiela replied blandly, "*Kabhi kisee bhai ney apni bhain sey kucchh manga hai*?" (Has a brother ever asked anything of his sister?). Bharat stayed on with us a couple of days after Shiela had left. One day he asked me if he could take my wife out for lunch and what would be a good place for them to eat. I scribbled the name of the restaurant, Tour d'Argent, the most expensive eatery in Paris. "Every taxi-driver knows where it is," I assured him, and told my wife, "This is your only chance to eat in Tour d'Argent."

The taxi-driver took them to the restaurant. Bharat examined the menu and the prices at the entrance. "This is far too expensive and there is nothing on the menu for a vegetarian," he exclaimed. They ate in a cheap bistro.

Bharat's generosity saved the breakup of the vast industrial empire built by Sir Shri Ram and doubled by Bharat and his brother Charat. There were many claimants. There was Savitri, the only child of Shri Ram's brother, Sir Shankar Lal. And there was Bansidhar, the son of Bharat's elder brother Murlidhar who had been killed in a plane crash at Karachi. Bharat gave them their legitimate shares and his brother Charat what he thought was due to him. Unlike other large business houses, the Shri Rams did not go into litigation. Bharat himself passed on his share of the business to his four sons and decided to lead a retired life with as much golf and good time as he could manage.

Before he could indulge himself in sport and good living, he developed heart trouble. His doctors told him to give up smoking. He did so without hesitation. Then his close friend Amarjeet Singh, whom he had helped to study in Cambridge University, died suddenly. Bharat was terribly shaken. "*Ab kitney din rah gayen hain hamaarey*? (How many days are left for us now?), he asked when we dropped in for a drink the last time. My wife replied, "Bharat, we'll go together hand in hand?" That cheered him up. "*Pukkee baat*?" (That's a promise?), he replied, putting out his hand. We decided to meet at least once a week, in his home or ours. That was many months ago.

12

Krishen Shungloo

Unequal contest: The great Indian novel that was never written.

The woman with the golden breasts never bared her orbs. After three or four attempts to write a novel, Shungloo simply gave up the idea. I came to the conclusion that people who think of titles of novels never get to write them.

I first saw him in 1937 in an examination centre in London. Both of us were hoping to get into the ICS. Neither of us did. He had come down from Oxford, I was from a humbler university and lowly rated King's College, London University. Two years later we met in Lahore. He had an Oxford degree, I an LL.B. from London and was a Barrister-at-law from the Inner Temple. He had no job, I had no clients.

We began spending our mornings at the coffee house where other briefless lawyers, would-be politicians and future winners of the Nobel Prize for literature foregathered to tear apart reputations of people who were doing better than us. Krishen Shungloo was as handsome a Kashmiri Pandit as I had ever met: tall, well-built, bespectacled and impeccably well-dressed in dark suits and his Oxford college tie. Also very soft-spoken and erudite. He was a chain smoker, and unknown to us, wrote poetry in English late into the night.

Shungloo lived in a joint family. He did not need to earn his livelihood and disdained work. All that changed with the partition of the country in August 1947. We found ourselves in Delhi. Shungloo got a job in All India Radio.. I got one in the Ministry of External Affairs. Shungloo acquired a wife (needless to say a Kashmiri Pandit) Sarojini, whom we called Bitto.

We resumed our friendship after I resigned from government service. By then I had a book to my credit: *The Mark of Vishnu and Other Stories*. We squared our score of one book each. A friendly rivalry developed between us. Who would write the next book? We dined in each other's homes, taking our food in tiffin carriers and a bottle of Indian whisky. On Sunday mornings we met for coffee at the Volga in Connaught Place. We did not gossip about people but about books.

Periodically Krishen Shungloo would get obsessed with the idea of writing a novel. He would apply for a month's leave, buy fancy notebooks, sharpen a dozen pencils and ask me to join him and his wife for coffee. Then through clouds of cigarette smoke, he would announce: "K. Singh I have taken leave to write a novel." We were duly impressed. Afte a few more puffs of smoke he would ask: "What do you thin of this as a title for a novel: *The Woman with Golde Breasts*?" We were doubly impressed.

"Sounds wonderful," I would reply. "What is it going t be about?" Shungloo would relax and reply: "*Woh to abhe sochenge*" (That I will have to think about). The woman wit the golden breasts never bared her orbs. After three or fo attempts to write a novel, Shungloo simply gave up the ide I came to the conclusion that people who think of titles novels never get to write them. Actually Krishen Shungloo was born lazy. We were together for two years when I joined All India Radio. He kept up a great pretence of being overworked and left office an hour after everyone else had gone. Actually he had no more work than I. It seldom took me more that half an hour to clear my table.

Our forty-year-old friendship came apart for reasons that baffle me. While Shungloo was unable to write books I was churning them out at the rate of two every year, being invited to writers' conferences and being written about in the papers. I looked forward to receiving a pat on my back from Krishen and Sarojini Shungloo. That pat never came. Instead I got the feeling that he resented the little success that came to me. I was hurt and dropped the Shungloos.

After retirement, Krishen took to a pattern of life that suited him best. He read books all mornings and played bridge in the afternoons and evenings. He only went out to the market to buy vegetables. I lost contact with him. Then one morning I was rung up by a common friend who told me that Krishen Shungloo returned from the bazaar, lay down on the sofa and died. Something inside me snapped. I drove out to his house in Maharani Bagh. He lay on the floor looking fast asleep. Would he snore again? Would he meet the girl with the golden breasts? My eyes filled with tears. I bade him farewell.

13

Charanjit Singh

With childish glee Charanjit came to show off his custom-built Rolls Royce; only it refused to start.

Charanjit was almost 30 years younger than me; he never read books and was devoutly religious and also very superstitious. He believed in astrology and miracles.... None of this meant anything to me. Nevertheless, we became friends. I became a kind of father-figure he turned to whenever he was troubled.

Some years ago I was in my home enjoying my evening Scotch and listening to taped *keertan* by Darshan Singh who had been my favourite *raagi* ever since I first heard him sing.

There was a knock at my door. It was Charanjit Singh, then member of the Lok Sabha, president of the New Delhi Municipal Committee, owner of Campa Cola — one of the wealthiest Sikhs in the country.

Our families had known each other since the 1920s when they settled in Delhi but they were not very close. Ours had been the leading Sikh family in Delhi with two knights and an uncle who had been a finance minister of Punjab and then Governor of Tamil Nadu.

Our fortunes were on the decline. Charanjit's father, Sardar Bahadur Mohan Singh, had, on the other hand, risen from a humble furniture maker to be the top builder in the city. He had got the franchise of Coca Cola, opened factories in all big cities of India and became a multi-millionaire. He built himself a palatial mansion in New Friends Colony and upon acquired a fleet of imported limousines.

We looked down upon the Mohan Singh family as *nouveau riche* upstarts; they looked down upon us as a decadent lot who had lost the ability to make money.

Mohan Singh had two sons, Daljit and Charanjit, and a clutch of daughters. One of Daljit's daughters was married to a distant relative.

Charanjit who had inherited drive and ambition was known to be arrogant. I for one had no desire to befriend him. I was surprised to see him come to my house.

I offered Charanjit a Scotch. He took it but was uneasy. "You listen to *Guru ki banee* while you are drinking liquor," he remarked. To him this was blasphemous.

"You try it sometime," I advised him. "You will enjoy the *keertan* much more." However, to spare him more embarrassment, I switched off the tape. He had come on business.

That morning Charanjit had come to the Rajya Sabha to listen to a debate on the anti-Sikh riots following the assassination of Mrs. Gandhi. He was the worst sufferer in Delhi: three of his Campa Cola plants had been wrecked by Hindu mobs. He had received no compensation and the machinery he had imported to replace what he had lost had been held up by Bombay Customs—obviously at the instance of a rival firm of soft-drink makers who hoped to capture the Delhi market from Charanjit's Campa Cola. In the debate I spoke with some passion against the callousness of the government in rehabilitating the Sikhs. Rajiv Gandhi got up to apologise for the government's tardiness in releasing blankets, sweaters, scarves and other garments sent by Sikh communities living abroad in my name.

That evening tons of woollen clothing were released to me to be distributed among victims of the Delhi violence.

"Why don't you help me to have my machinery released?" asked Charanjit after explaining what had happened to him.

"You never asked me," I replied. "And you are a member of Parliament and a friend of Mrs. Gandhi's family."

"I've tried but nothing has been done," he replied somewhat woebegone.

I knew he had been giving money to the Gandhi family and had a car reserved for them whenever they wanted it. I promised to do my best.

By sheer chance Rajiv Gandhi summoned me to his chamber to discuss the rehabilitation of Sikh victims of the 1984 violence. Home Minister Buta Singh was present. So was the portly Unnikrishnan whom Charanjit claimed was his friend. Buta Singh made a statement about how much had been done.

I contradicted him at every step and specially mentioned the case of Charanjit Singh. That evening Charanjit's machinery was released by the Customs on orders of the Prime Minister.

The next day Charanjit came with a large bouquet of gladioli to thank me. He had heard from Unnikrishnan what had transpired in the Prime Minister's office. Unnikrishnan said he had supported me; he had not even opened his mouth.

"I am told you give Members of Parliament large sums of money to get your work done. You fob me off with a few flowers," I said.

He laughed and replied, "If I knew you take money I would have given it to you a long time ago."

Thus began an unlikely relationship. Charanjit was almost 30 years younger than me; he never read books and was devoutly religious and also very superstitious. He believed in astrology and miracles. Once a month, he went to see some Santji near Ludhiana and had *akhand paths* and *keertans* in his home regularly.

None of this meant anything to me. Nevertheless, we became friends. I became a kind of father-figure he turned to whenever he was troubled. His ravishingly beautiful wife Harjeet (Bubbles) and he became regular visitors to our flat.

He made me a director of Le Meridien hotel in New Delhi.

On his way back home he would drop in on me and ring up his wife to come over. In some ways their friendship with us brought the couple closer to each other.

Charanjit loved living in style and was generous beyond belief. In Delhi we spent weekends together in his spacious farm house near village Chattarpur. Whenever I went to Calcutta, Madras, Kanpur or Chandigarh, I had to stay with his sisters. Whenever I was in London I stayed in his apartment near Marble Arch. In Frankfurt with his close friends Ella and Romesh Singh.

He loaded me with gifts — the most expensive gifts I had ever received. Two gold and silver Cartier pens worth Rs. 15,000 each. I had to plead with him not to give me a gold Cartier wrist watch. All I could give him in return were books. And books were of no use to him.

In later years I noted Charanjit getting irritable and short-tempered. Neither his wife nor his other friends had the nerve to tell him that. It was left to me to tell him the unpleasant truth. Once he embarrassed me at a press conference in Le Meridien where he asked me to preside.

After a short question and answer session he announced to the pressmen that he was taking Prime Minister V.P. Singh to court. He had litigation in his blood.

Every minor quarrel which could have been settled by a little give-and-take was taken by him to court. He must have spent a fortune paying lawyers' fees. And was in turn fed by stories of their success in pursuing his cases — none of which was true.

Charanjit loved cars and collected them like a child collects toys. Despite owning Mercedes Benzes and Toyotas, he arrived at my flat one evening to show me his latest purchase: it was a custom-built Rolls Royce. Much to his chagrin when he was to drive off, the car refused to start. My son-in-law who was admiring it could not resist quipping, "Charanjit, shall we push your Rolls Royce to get it going?"

I have little doubt that the extravagant style of life and business worries told on Charanjit's health. When his brother Daljit died in his sleep, Charanjit went into a deep depression. A few months later he suffered his first heart attack and was put in the intensive care ward of Escorts Hospital. Doctors assured him that they had succeeded in dissolving a clot going towards his heart and discharged him. He was advised not to receive visitors and to take a few rounds of his gardens every evening. My wife and I were the only people allowed to see him. We did so every evening. The last time we were together he had his tailor over to narrow his trousers and his coats as he had lost his paunch.

He was very pleased with himself. "When are you going to England next?" he asked me. "I have no immediate plans," I replied. "I am a freeloader. Whenever someone sends me a ticket and offers me five-star hospitality, I go. No one has asked me," I replied.

"We will go together. I want to have my heart rechecked in the United States. These Johnnies here know nothing about the heart. I will look after the travel and all else. We will fly in the Concorde," he said grandly.

That night he had a massive heart attack. On his way to the Escorts Hospital his heart stopped beating.

I was told about it in the early hours of the next morning and hurried to his house to be with his wife. This was on my son Rahul's birthday. He was expecting Rajiv Gandhi at the party in our flat. Rajiv went to condole with Harjeet and then came to us. Only the Charanjits were not there and my heart was full of grief.

14

N. Iqbal Singh

Small, effeminate Iqqy Singh
went on to become a big
ladies man.

"What about sex?" I asked him. "No problem. I have tribal women on my staff. Tribals have no hang-ups about sex." I marvelled at Iqqy's versatility. On his posting back home he produced an illustrated book on the tribes of the Andaman Islands. The girls had nothing on them except beads.

He was the smallest, the most dapperly dressed and effeminate looking Sikh in my days in Government College, Lahore. He could not have been more than 5 feet 3 inches tall. He wore a neat turban but instead of coloured ribbon showing underneath its angle, he had a lock of his own hair to serve the same purpose. His one eye was slightly larger than the other; it looked very odd under his rimless glasses. The one thing that struck everyone as very odd was that though he was in his early twenties his voice had not broken and sounded like a woman's. Most boys called him *choochee*. His friends, among whom I was one, called him Iqqy. No one knew what the letter N he put before his name stood for. He was as far from being a ladies man as any man I knew. Evidently I did not sense any masculinity latent in his small frame.

Iqqy was about the most popular student in the college. He was not particularly good in his studies, played no games nor took part in social activities. The secret of his popularity was that he was a good listener and ever willing to share other people's problems. He never seemed to have any of his own. Nor did he run down anyone.

We soon became friends. Although a couple of years senior to me, we made it a point to go to the mess together for our meals and he was usually in our party which included Chetan Anand to go to the cinema which we did at least once every week. Those days Tarzan's series with Johnny Weismuller playing the ape-man were eagerly awaited. We also never missed a film which had any of the Barrymoore family, Greta Garbo or Norma Shearer appearing in them. Hindi films had not yet made the grade but we did not miss any with K.L. Saigal or Prithviraj Kapoor. Together we saw Devika Rani with Himanshu Rai and Sadhana Bose who almost seduced Chetan when we went to her hotel room to get her autograph.

I lost contact with Iqqy and my other Government College friends when I went off to England to study for the Bar and LL.B. in London University. I returned home in 1939 and resumed my friendship. Chetan and Iqqy were two friends to attend my marriage. Iqqy disgraced himself by getting very drunk and throwing up on the carpet. Neither my parents nor my wife ever forgot or forgave his misbehaviour.

It was after I returned to Lahore to practise law that Iqqy came back into my life. His voice had changed and became masculine. He had joined All India Radio as a talks producer: he occasionally invited me to broadcast. He had also developed interest in women. Among those he met regularly was the painter Amrita Shergil (who gave him some of her paintings) and her closest friend Helen Chaman Lal. Rumour had it that Amrita granted Iqqy favours she did not grant to her other lovers. Iqqy always maintained a mysterious silence about his relations with women. I could not fathom the secret of Iqqy's success with people who mattered. It was always a one-way traffic. He was always descending on them. And was welcomed. He rarely ever returned hospitality. He lived a shabby, one-room bachelor existence. Come to think of it, whether in Lahore or Delhi, I never knew where Iqqy really hung out.

In the summer of 1951 Iqqy spent a month or more with me in London. I had resigned my job in India House, my family had returned to India and I was living in a two-bedroom basement flat in Highgate. I had stocked enough duty-free liquor to last me six months. I planned to stay on in England to finish a book I was writing. Iqqy had sold one of Amrita Shergil's paintings which gave him enough money to pay for his sea-passage to England and back. The day after he arrived I decided to throw a party to welcome him. It turned out to be quite a binge which exposed yet another aspect of Iqqy's character.

Among my guests was a starlet, Jennifer Dawson, who lived two floors above me. She had become a regular visitor. Whenever she saw light through my window when she returned home from the theatre, she rang my bell to have her nightcap and a chat. Jennifer was a very pretty girl. And very proper. I never risked taking liberties with her for fear of losing her friendship. I loaded her with gifts and compliments but never touched her.

The party went on late in the night and most of my guests were drunk by the time they left. Iqqy who didn't have to go anywhere was more drunk than others. Jennifer who was very careful with how much she took stayed on chatting merrily. Iqqy got up and planted himself on the arm of Jennifer's chair and began to fondle her hair. I spoke to him in Punjabi to stop bothering her. Jennifer got up from her armchair and sat down on another. Iqqy followed her and renewed his amours, this time kissing her hair: her hair was most kissable. I again told him in Punjabi not to pester the girl. "Please tell your friend to behave himself," pleaded Jennifer. But Iqqy ignored our pleas and followed Jennifer around the room from chair to chair. In desperation I asked Jennifer to return to her flat. She seemed reluctant to leave. The charade went on for another half-an-hour till I almost pushed Jennifer out of my apartment. I was very angry with Iqqy as I feared Jennifer would never come to see me again. I said nothing to him that night because he was beyond understanding. After I retired to bed, I heard him retch and throw up in the bathroom. Iqqy could never hold his drink.

The next morning he had a terrible hangover. I reprimanded him for his bad behaviour. "Oh" he exclaimed innocently, "what did I do?" Then he focused his eyes on a painting of my ten-year-old son and asked, "That's Rahul; who did it?" I told him "Patricia Angadi; she is the English wife of Angadi."

Iqqy nodded his head and seemed to doze off for a few seconds. He raised his head, looked at the painting and asked again, "Who did that?" I told him again about Patricia Angadi. A couple of moments later Iqqy's attention was again drawn towards Rahul's painting. "That's Rahul, isn't it? Who painted it?" I screamed with exasperation: "For the third and the last time, it was painted by Patricia Angadi. She is an English woman married to an Indian." The I let him have it about the way he had behaved towards Jennifer. He listened in silence. I also left a note under Jennifer's door apologising for Iqqy's conduct and pleading with her not to stop dropping in as usual.

How wrong I was I discovered a couple of days later. I was working by my window when I saw Iqqy go out of my apartment. A moment later Jennifer Dawson came down and joined him. The two took a bus to go out for dinner.

When I returned to Delhi, Iqqy was holding a senior position in All India Radio. He was appointed Station Officer at Port Blair. I wondered how an essentially social character would survive in the tropical wilderness of the Andamans. On one of his holiday visits I asked him how he was doing. "Very well. I am my own master. I am collecting material on the Onges who inhabit the Islands," he replied. "What about sex?" I asked him. "No problem. I have tribal women on my staff. Tribals have no hang-ups about sex." I marvelled at Iqqy's versatility. On his posting back home he produced an illustrated book on the tribes of the Andaman Islands. The girls had nothing on them except beads and tiny jock-straps to cover their pubes. They were as ugly as Australian Aborigines.

I don't recall when Iqqy got rid of his turban and long hair and began to sport neatly trimmed and pointed French style beard. He looked more dapper than before. For some months in Delhi he escorted Meher Moos of Air India.

This cherry blossom Bawaji had explored the South Pole and other godforsaken places all over the world. The two made their rounds together to homes of Soli Sorabji, Shakuntala Masani and Helen Chaman Lal. They dropped in on me once or twice. But since I did not welcome visitors who come without prior information, I was dropped from their list.

Iqqy sold another Amrita Shergil. And took another holiday in Europe dividing his time between the nobility and the well-to-do he had befriended earlier. After retiring from All India Radio on a very modest pension Iqqy had to find a place to stay and earn money to live in the style he was used to. For a while he moved into his sister's *pension* in Bombay to help her with its running. They shifted to Chandigarh where he now lives. He wrote a biography of Amrita Shergil.

I thought I could put some money his way by suggesting to Deepti Naval who was planning to make a documentary on Amrita that she use Iqqy's manuscript but he snubbed me for daring to suggest that he do so. I was very put off with his brusque dismissal.

His book on Amrita Shergil was published. I have no idea what he got for it. He writes an occasional article for *The Tribune* and helps in editing some Punjab Government journals. Evidently he earns enough to live comfortably.

From friends in Chandigarh I also learn that Iqqy now returns hospitality and entertains people at home. The last time I was in Chandigarh, I ran into him at an exhibition of drawings, blueprints, and pictures on the genesis of the city. He extended an invitation to me to have a drink. He must have been relieved to learn that I would not be able to make it as I had to be present at a party given for me by my host. "Where are you staying?" he asked me.

"At the Haryana Raj Bhawan," I replied.

"Oh?" he exclaimed. Dismissing me as an upstart and a snob.

15

Satendra Singh

As the cliché goes, Satendra was a man larger than life.

He had been an Akali and then a communist — or perhaps it was the other way round. I was also not sure about the sexual prowess he boasted of. I know one hot Sunday afternoon in June I invited him for lunch to meet a Maharashtrian girl I had met in the States.... After lunch I asked Satendra to drop her at her barsati. *The next day he rang up and asked me her name. "You know I accompanied her to the* barsati *and there without as much as a by your leave I took her to bed. It was very hot but we continued to make love till sunset. I never got to know her name."*

I cannot recall when I first met Satendra Singh. It must have been at least thirty years ago and probably at the India Coffee House in Connaught Place. He was a daily visitor and held durbar every morning with other regulars. As in coffee houses all over India most regulars were semi-employed journalists and small-time politicians. With relays of cups of coffee they slander everyone in the public eye from the President and Prime Minister down to lady members of the municipality. Satendra knew the private lives of everyone who mattered.

My first reaction to him was adverse. He was a tall, paunchy Sardar, wearing an ill-fitting small turban, with puffed out cheeks, thick glasses and a stubble of a beard. People were drawn to him because he was a good raconteur of bawdy jokes and had an incredibly large repertoire of Urdu and Punjabi poetry. He had a computer-like memory for dates, names and figures. At the time he was working for a weekly English newspaper which enjoyed respect in political circles but had a very small circulation. Satendra was devoted to its editor Professor Ram Singh whom he rated to be the best editor in the country. After Ram Singh's death, Satendra transferred his adoration to Prem Bhatia.

I realised there was more to Satendra than I had thought when he married the prettiest girl in New Delhi. I had eyed her for the role of the heroine in my novel *Train to Pakistan* (it was never filmed). They made a strange couple: he an ungainly Sardar, perhaps the ugliest man around, she a petite Hindu girl with sparkling dark eyes. She could have married a handsome rich man but she married Satendra who had neither looks nor much of bank balance. He was also known to be a hard drinker and prone to violence. The marriage proved to be a misalliance. After she had borne him two daughters, she walked out on him following a violent quarrel. Satendra was devastated. And vengeful. It was then that he turned to me for advice and comfort. I persuaded him to give his wife the divorce she sought. He was freed of his matrimonial obligations, he could drink as much as he liked and there were lots of women willing to become his mistresses.

Satendra became a regular visitor in my house. As was his habit when he made a friend, he befriended the entire family. He soon became a favourite with my wife, daughter and son-in-law. At least once a week he dined with us. My wife rationed his drink to three tots of rum before dinner. He took the restriction in good grace but I was certain he went home and resumed drinking.

I was uneasy with his politics. He had been an Akali and then a communist — or perhaps it was the other way round. I was also not sure about the sexual prowess he boasted of. I know one hot Sunday afternoon in June I invited him for lunch to meet a Maharashtrian girl I had met in the States. She was a wager, this girl with protruding teeth and thick glasses, as sexless in appearance as any I had met. After lunch I asked Satendra to drop her at her *barsati*. The next day he rang me up and asked me her name. "You know I accompanied her to the *barsati* and there without as much as a by your leave I took her to bed. It was very hot but we continued to make love till sunset. I never got to know her name."

I did not see the girl again; so I could not verify Satendra's claim. But periodically he visited me in Bombay and a lady friend of his came from Pune to spend a couple of days with him. He took the keys of my apartment and returned them to me in the evening as I was about to leave office. When I got home I could see that the rum I stocked for him had been well-consumed and my bed bore evidence of having been bashed about.

We resumed our friendship when I returned to Delhi. He was drinking more than ever. On a couple of occasions he bashed his car driving home at night and had to be hospitalised. Then suddenly he suffered a mild heart attack and had to be put in intensive care.

When I went to see him in hospital I took a wad of currency notes to shift him from the general ward to a private room. President Giani Zail Singh had been to see him earlier that morning and unknown to him slipped an envelope with

Rs 5,000 under his pillow. When my wife did the same, he was overcome with emotion and began to sob.

After his family had ditched him, his friends gathered around him. Satendra had the gift of friendship. Despite his enormous learning (he had amassed quite a library which he had procured from me) and ability to handle the English language, Satendra did not devote much time to routine work. Prem Bhatia was compelled to terminate his contract with *The Tribune*. Satendra was very hurt.

At one time our friendship almost came to an end. He was turning more and more to Khalistanis and went out of his way to pick up quarrels with my Hindu friends. Angry words passed between us. He was contrite and apologised: "You are my only friend, don't drop me," he pleaded. I did not drop him despite my dislike of his communal views. At every party we gave or was given for me, we made it a point to invite Satendra. The last one was at the Maurya Sheraton for the release of my book *Nature Watch*.

He came to my apartment to get a lift to the hotel. He was smelling of drink. I had to switch off the airconditioner and let down the glass panes to get fresh air.

At the party I saw him go from one group to another embracing men and women and tossing in pegs of Scotch. I had to leave early as I had to catch the Himalayan Queen very early next morning. I went to Satendra to ask him to come along. "You go," he said. "I'll get a lift from Mala and Ravi (my daughter and son-in-law)."

That is the last I saw of him. It was the day after that I read in *The Tribune* that Satendra had died in his sleep. I got the details from my daughter. She and her husband had to help him out of the car and to deposit him in his flat. The next day Satendra's servant had come to our apartment, and finding us gone had called on Mala.

The sahib had bolted his door from inside and was not responding to his knocking. My daughter rang up Satendra's brother-in-law Inder Malhotra. They got the police to break open the door. Satendra was lying dead in his bed. A half-empty bottle of rum lay under his bed.

Satendra was, as the cliché goes, a man larger than life. His going left a deafening silence in my life.

Also by
Khushwant Singh
Sex, Scotch & Scholarship
Selected Writings

In this anthology you can look forward to some talk of sex, a little of Scotch and much scholarship. The collection attempts to mirror the author's concerns and passions — his love of nature, his anguish over the situation in Punjab, his interest in religions of the world and his scholarly research of the one into which he was born, Sikhism.

The highlight of this book, however, is the expansive, autobiographical opening piece written in Khushwant's characteristically candid style and perhaps the most complete self-portrait he has yet painted.

Quite simply, quintessential Khushwant.

Khushwant Singh is a man of many parts... unique in many ways. There isn't another like him. Probably there never will be. His writings are like a Scandinavian breakfast buffet-smorgasbord — so varied they are in style, content and gravity... one may like him or hate him, but one thing about him is beyond denial. Like the Qutab Minar or India Gate, he has become an institution.

— *M.V. Kamath*

Khushwant Singh is an engima... he will continue to be read... he will continue to regale and shock viewers with his belief that "there is life on the udder side..."

— *The Hindustan Times*

... the book is a good buy; it contains a sample of the wide range of subjects on which Khushwant has written, is highly readable and thoroughly enjoyable.

— *Indian Review of Books*

Also by
Khushwant Singh
My Bleeding Punjab

Those who want Khalistan, can have it in Ecuador, they can have it in the South Pole but they will not have it in India.

— Khushwant Singh

"On the 1st of *Baisakh*, 13th April 1978, celebrated as New Year's day in the Punjab calendar, Jarnail Singh Bhindranwale exploded like a nuclear bomb. It not only shook overfed Punjabis out of their slumbers but the fallout continues to plague the rest of the country even today." This indeed is the tragic story of the troubled and terror-torn state of Punjab. Today, the complexities of the problem seem not only to be defying all solutions but at periodic intervals, pose a very real threat to the integrity of the nation. This book, in parts unashamedly emotional, lucidly traces the history of the problem, detailing the grievances and resentments of the Punjabis since Independence and touching upon all the major developments.

What makes this volume special is the author's personal involvement, apparent on every page, and reflecting his views on Punjab politics and the mess made by "narrow-minded Akali leaders, on the one side, and the deliberately mischievous politics of the Central Government," on the other. The unfortunate result is there for all to see: all progress in the most progressive state of India is at a standstill, its agricultural and industrial economy lies ruined and its administration and judiciary have been reduced to shambles. What is perhaps more disturbing is the fact that there is still no hope of a solution on the horizon.

This book is a must for anyone who wants an in-depth understanding of the present impasse.

Also by
Khushwant Singh
Need For a New Religion in India & Other Essays

This book is a collection of essays on a wide range of subjects — The Language of Love and Lust, The Monsoon in Literature, Ghosts and Life Hereafter and other Laughing Matters, and a little essay which sets out a brilliant blueprint for a new, practical ritual-free religion, more relevant perhaps in today's times than ever before.

The second half of the book should be of particular interest to students of literature and readers who wish to know more about some of the greatest authors of our times.

Written in his familiar, readable, easily comprehensible style, Khushwant brings to each subject a wealth of knowledge and information.

Extremely erudite and readable.... Anyone interested in the making of literature will profit from reading and re-reading these pieces. Those who are horrified by recent trends in the country, would do well to commit to memory the title piece — a piece that should form the centrepiece of the manifestos of every political party and the foundation of the thought processes of every thinking Indian.

— *Indian Express*

Forthcoming

from

Khushwant Singh
Nature Watch

This is the diary of a nature lover patterned after the traditional *Baramasi* of Indian poets. It tells you of trees, flowers, fruits, birds, snakes, insects and animals to be seen during the twelve months of the year. It also tells of the many fairs and festivals celebrated in the country; how clouds are formed and what their shapes and movements mean; why hailstorms come in spring and early summer and not in winter; how birds communicate with each other and why their calls vary with the seasons. With the descriptions of nature are included poems on natural phenomena by poets like Kalidasa, Guru Nanak, Meer Taqi Meer, Mirza Ghalib, Akbar Ilahabadi, Rabindranath Tagore, Rudyard Kipling and many others.